The church, Christian institutions, and our w
who are people after God's own heart. *The Fi*
excellent and essential reference for all Christ
presents these five phases in a way that guides l … to lead in a godly and biblical way. It is not a book that can be read just once, but it is one that needs to be read again and again as it helps leaders to evaluate themselves continuously. I highly recommend this book as a companion for every person in a leadership position.

The Most Rev. Dr. Mouneer Hanna Anis
Archbishop, Episcopal Anglican Diocese of Egypt

Leadership is much like life. Life can appear infinitely complex, yet it can also be reduced to simple formulas. Likewise, entire libraries exist devoted to leadership, yet people who are successful at it can boil it down to a handful of fundamental behaviors. Justyn Terry has masterfully done this. Both a successful scholar and practitioner, Terry has reduced leadership to five essential practices. Each has enormous ramifications and is ignored at great cost. Modern society, as well as the church, is desperately clamoring for good leadership. The stakes are high. The challenges are herculean. This book will help.

Richard Blackaby
President of Blackaby Ministries International
Co-author, *Spiritual Leadership,* and *Called to Be God's Leader*

I cannot recommend Justyn Terry's book highly enough for anyone in leadership! In an age which idolizes leadership and leadership books and formulae, this is refreshingly authentic. Deeply biblical, humble, and insightful. Full of practical wisdom. Packed with fresh clarity and honest case studies covering the five phases of Leadership Life Cycle, complete with questions for reflection. Justyn is an insightful teacher and practitioner, rooted in Scripture and the need for the fruit of the Spirit and Christ-like character formation. Read it!

Rt Revd Jill Duff, DPhil
Anglican Bishop of Lancaster, UK

It is so good to be reminded that being called to leadership is a responsibility which we are given only for a season – and that that season, if we are to be faithful stewards, calls for different approaches over its lifespan. Justyn Terry's book contains much biblical and practical wisdom for how we can start and end well in each responsibility that comes to us, growing and being prepared for the next season.

Paul Harcourt
National Leader, New Wine England

In a season in which Christian leaders are being stretched in new ways, Justyn Terry's work stands out as a beacon, calling us to mark our time in measured seasons, each one informed by the witness of the biblical text. With the skilled hindsight of a seasoned pastor, he draws on examples from his own ministry to illuminate the challenges leaders face, and he prayerfully and practically offers guidance which translates well across geographical and denominational divides. This is a book to which readers can return time and time again as they seek to discern God's vision and leading in their own context.

Rev. Tracey Henry
Presbyterian Church (USA)

Leadership is complex. Anyone who suggests otherwise has never led anything significant. But complex doesn't mean opaque. This practical guide takes us through the process of leading well from arriving to leaving in five overlapping phases. Woven through with personal stories from his leadership in a church and seminary, reflection on biblical themes, and insights from contemporary authors, Terry acts as a wise companion on the journey. If you know someone starting out on the complex journey of leadership, do them a favour and give them this book. They will thank you.

James Lawrence
Leadership Principal, Church Pastoral Aid Society (CPAS)

I am very grateful to have gotten to know Justyn Terry while attending a program at Oxford several years back. One who honours both people and results, Terry has led with integrity of heart and skilful hands. He is a safe leader who is competent, reliable and relational – a very rare combination! I highly recommend this book and have no doubt that this will be a profitable read.

Rachel Ong
CEO, ROHEI Corporation
Member of Parliament, Singapore

This book is a wonderful distillation of practical wisdom gained from long experience of hands-on leadership, allied to a good deal of biblical and theoretical reflection, all with the clear aim of equipping God's people better for faithful missional ministry. This simple exposition of five priorities for Christian leaders is laced with helpful suggestions as to how they might be worked out in the life of a local church leader. Justyn Terry's generous spirit and infectious confidence in God's power and equipping have led him to produce a book which will inspire faith and hope both in those who are setting out on the journey of leadership and those more experienced practitioners who want to see their own leadership sharpened and refreshed.

Ian Parkinson
Associate Archdeacon,
Transition Enabler, Diocese of Sheffield, UK

A thought-provoking resource, *The Five Phases of Leadership* defines the fundamentals of a leader's life cycle with a practiced finesse! Dwelling not so much on leadership-managerial skills and strategies, the heart of Justyn Terry's book focuses on five phases of leadership, namely, establishing trust, cultivating leaders, discerning vision, implementing plans, and transitioning out. Drawing on his leadership experience both in the church and out, Terry has woven into the book biblical values that are core to any biblical leader. The "life cycle of a leader" locus makes it a global resource – an essential and relevant read for all pastors and leaders around the world! I have enjoyed the book myself by my friend Terry, and I know many others will too!

Finny Philip, PhD
Principal, Filadelfia Bible College, Udaipur, India

The Five Phases of Leadership

The Five Phases of Leadership

An Overview for Christian Leaders

Revised and Expanded Edition

Justyn Terry

Published 2021 by Langham Global Library
An imprint of Langham Publishing
www.langhampublishing.org

Langham Publishing and its imprints are a ministry of Langham Partnership

Langham Partnership
PO Box 296, Carlisle, Cumbria, CA3 9WZ, UK
www.langham.org

Previously published by Whitchurch Publishing, 2016, under the same title.

ISBNs:
978-1-83973-068-9 Print
978-1-83973-457-1 ePub
978-1-83973-458-8 Mobi
978-1-83973-459-5 PDF

British Library Cataloguing-in-Publication Data
A catalogue record for this book is available from the British Library.

ISBN: 978-1-83973-068-9

Cover & Book Design: projectluz.com

Contents

Foreword

Leadership matters, and it matters a lot." This opening sentence of Justyn Terry's introduction firmly but politely indicates his agenda, his character and his method of presentation in this book. Order can be brought out of chaos, clarity out of confusion, mission out of maintenance, and growth out of stagnation. All this can be, and has been, achieved if the leader acts gently but firmly with honesty, love, patience and discernment.

Leadership is a subject about which much has been written in recent years, but often this has been done in a secular or business context. A distinctive contribution of this book is that it is written by an experienced leader from a clear Christian perspective, and yet the content and methods which Justyn Terry sets forth are valid and valuable in any church or organization, whether religious or secular. This is a book whose ideas have been refined in the fire of personal experience and which contains many examples drawn primarily from the author's years spent as Vicar of St Helen's Church, London, and as Principal of Trinity School for Ministry, Pittsburgh, USA. This revised edition also draws on his subsequent time spent as Vice-Principal of Wycliffe Hall, Oxford, thereby showing how the same teaching is equally useful for a person in a supportive leadership role.

It is Terry's contention that there are five phases of leadership: establish trust, cultivate leaders, discern vision, implement plans, and transition out. These units are not mutually exclusive: there is a lot of overlap between them. The need to establish trust is basic: all leadership depends on the fostering of a trustworthy character. The main ingredients for establishing such a trust are to be found in the description of the mature Christian character in Galatians 5:22–23. Developing trust never ends, but the leader must find other leaders, or potential leaders, in order to expand the sphere of influence and to accomplish the mission (2 Tim 2:2). Discerning the vision, together with the purpose and core values, is time consuming and demanding, but its value is priceless. Without a clear vision the way ahead is clothed in mist. Implementing the plans needed to fulfil the vision is the longest section in the book, as dangers are pointed out, and the strategies and tactics, including the need to manage people, money and time, are fully discussed with many helpful examples.

When the time comes for the leader to leave, the transitioning out must be handled well if all the work done in the previous years is not to be undone. Discerning when to leave is difficult, and it is easy to fall into the temptation to rush away too soon, or to stay too long. The author continues to offer helpful, practical advice here too, as ever citing examples and explaining his thoughts with clarity and in a lucid and engaging style.

Justyn Terry is clear that Christian leadership is a great privilege and a formidable challenge, but in his overview of the different times and elements which are involved, he has given to the church and to the world a highly valuable tool which will be of great benefit for all about to take up leadership for the first time and also for those who have already begun the task. The call to leadership is a gift from God, and it is to God that great thanksgiving is owed for the call and for his unending faithfulness and provision, as we continue to rely on him and on the empowerment of his Holy Spirit.

The Most Revd Dr Benjamin A. Kwashi
Archbishop of the Province of Jos, and Bishop of Jos, Nigeria

Preface

This book started life in two places, like a child of two parents. One was a lecture I gave about church leadership at Trinity School for Ministry, a theological college, or seminary, in Pittsburgh, USA. It was based on my time leading St Helen's Church in North Kensington, London, and aimed to provide an overview of that experience from start to finish. The other was a series of short after-chapel addresses that I gave while I was leading Trinity School for Ministry, offering brief weekly tips on different aspects of leadership and management. I was trying to distil lessons I had learned about leadership at St Helen's, at Trinity, and as an international marketing manager in the electronics industry prior to ordination. Several students and faculty colleagues encouraged me to write them up for a wider audience, and here is the result.

At the heart of this book is the belief that there are five phases of leadership: establish trust, cultivate leaders, discern vision, implement plans, and transition out. As we will see, these are not five neatly separated units, since there is a lot of overlap between them. Nor is it a one-size-fits-all formula for leadership. It is, instead, an attempt to identify the main elements of leadership to help leaders see what stage they are at and what might be expected to come next. I will describe each phase as briefly as I can and arrange the material in such a way that you can easily pass over things that are already familiar. I know that leaders tend to be busy people who want every moment to count.

There are, of course, many books on leadership, often focusing on the character and skills that make for a good leader, or on the various styles of leadership. What is offered here is an overview of leadership, describing each of the seasons it typically involves. By looking at the normal life cycle of leadership, we may see why the many character traits and skills of leadership matter. My hope is that this approach will draw together what can seem like rather disparate elements of leadership by focusing on the leader's overall task.

So this is a book by a practitioner for practitioners. It is not so much lessons learned in the leadership library, as skills sharpened in the school of stewardship. Nor is this the leadership experience of someone running vast organizations, which relatively few leaders get to do. It is a reflection on the regular life of leadership to which I think all leaders can relate. The contribution I hope to make is that of a theologian who is used to trying to see how the different parts of a complex subject are related to one another. In many ways, it was my desire to understand how things fit together in the life of a leader that drew me to write this book in the first place: How does the need to develop trust relate to the practical challenges of spotting leaders, or to developing a vision? Why does it matter that I show patience when I can see so clearly what needs to be changed? What should be in place before I begin to think about moving to a new position? I wanted to see the wood for the trees in the world of leadership, so that I could appreciate the part played by each tree and what role it had in the wider wood.

It is a book for anyone in leadership, not just those in overall leadership. I wasn't sure if I could say that when I wrote the first edition. I wondered how useful it would be for someone in leadership but not in the overall leadership spot, as is the case for a great many leaders. It turns out that I am in such a position now myself. On my return to England from America, I became vice-principal, or vice-president, of a theological college in Oxford: Wycliffe Hall. It has been a joy to bring lessons learned as a principal, or president, of a theological college in one part of the world to support another principal of a theological college in a different part of the world. As I have been revising this book, I have therefore had the chance to think about leadership from my current experience as a supporting leader, and have seen that the same five phases of leadership apply here too. It is still a matter of establishing trust, cultivating leaders, discerning vision, implementing plans and knowing when to transition out, although that discerning of vision in particular needs to be subject to the overall leader's guidance and shaping.

Three other quick things before we get started: First, I write this as a Christian and expect this book to be used mainly by Christian leaders, but it is not for them alone. I believe these principles have wider application, so I hope even those unfamiliar with the Christian faith will find them helpful. Second, I think leadership is more caught than taught, so I recommend you look for leadership mentors who can help you grow as a leader. And third, I use short case studies not to suggest "this is the way things should be done," but just to say "this is how it was done – rightly or wrongly." Leaders can learn from examples of both success and failure.

Finally, I owe many people a debt of gratitude for helping to bring this book to publication. In the first edition it was Christopher Klukas, Director of Whitchurch Publishing, Pittsburgh, USA, who oversaw the project. I am also grateful to those who read the manuscript and gave me excellent feedback on it: Megan Carey, Geoff Chapman, Anne Cowley, David Drake, Karen Getz, Austin Gohn, John Guest, Mary Hays, Bill Henry, Steve Palmer, David Pennylegion,

John Rodgers, Scott Santibanez, Laurie and Mary Thompson, and my wife, Cathy Terry.

This revised and expanded edition builds on comments from those who used the first edition of this book, whether for entering into new leadership roles or as seasoned leaders refining their skills. I am very grateful to Pieter Kwant, director of Langham Literature, for encouraging me to rework *The Five Phases of Leadership* not only to incorporate those insights, but to make more substantial changes so it can be of greater use to Christian leaders around the world. My eleven years in the USA supplied numerous opportunities to meet international church leaders who came to Pittsburgh or invited me to preach and teach in their home countries, and this international dimension has been very exciting for me. Pieter connected me with Finny Philip, Principal of Filadelfia Bible College, Udaipur, and Paul Swarup, Presbyter in Charge, Cathedral Church of the Redemption, Delhi. They have been a great help in developing the book, especially through Finny's visit to Oxford bringing his and Paul's thoughts on it, so it could include insights from an Indian and Majority World perspective.

I also had the chance to teach these principles at the Anglican Leadership Institute in South Carolina, USA, in January 2018, to leaders from around the Anglican Communion, including clergy, archdeacons and bishops from Brazil, Burundi, Ghana, Indonesia, Malawi, Nigeria, South Sudan, Tanzania, Uganda, the UK and the USA. Each of them brought unique insights and helped me rethink the material in this book, and I want to thank them for the part they played: Mike Adegbile, Francis Barongo, Eraste Bigirimana, Gyordano Brasilino, Ali Calvin, Henok Hariyanto, James Kennedy, Godwin Makabi, Francis Matumba, Joram Ntakije, Sam Parddy, Matthew Taban Peter and Greg Snyder. It was a marvellous privilege to spend a week with them. There were fascinating accounts of the challenges they faced and of lessons learned from how they exercised their leadership. I am grateful to have the benefit of their wisdom in this new edition. I am also thankful for the feedback from Trevor Rayment, who read a draft of the revised book. Many thanks go to Archbishop Ben Kwashi for all his inspirational leadership and for writing the foreword. Any shortcomings are of course my own, but I am sure this revised edition is much stronger for the contribution each of these leaders has made to it.

Finally, I am deeply grateful to the people of St Helen's Church, North Kensington, and Trinity School for Ministry, Pittsburgh, where I learned so many leadership lessons, and to Laurence Gamlen, who was such a help as our consultant at St Helen's. I am also very thankful to Wycliffe Hall, for allowing me study leave to work on this revision, and to my wife, Cathy, for her remarkable wisdom and steadfast support through all these years of learning to be a leader. I dedicate this book to her.

Oxford, UK

Introduction

Leadership matters, and it matters a lot. Everyone is affected by leadership in countless ways, whether in their homes, workplaces, communities or nation. Leaders make things happen. They perceive where an organization is, discern a vision for a better future, and use their influence to develop plans to get there. As leadership mentor John Guest says, "Nothing moves in the right direction without leadership."[1] So we need lots of leaders, and we need them to lead well. When they do a good job, leaders can make life better for many people; but when they do badly, a lot of people get hurt. So it is important that we all take leadership seriously, and each try to play our part in promoting the growth of numerous strong leaders. We want leaders who use their God-given gifts for the widest possible good. We want them to grow in their leadership, learning lessons that will enable them to lead with ever greater skill and effectiveness. And we want them to be a huge blessing to those they serve, and to bring glory to God. It is in everyone's interest to see leaders lead well.

My own interest in leadership goes back to an early age. I was always fascinated by leaders, whether they were my parents, teachers, pastors, or the many leaders I heard about through the media. I tried to understand them and what they did. When I first took up a leadership role as a teenager in a school Christian Union, I attempted to emulate them. I also started reading books about leadership, such as J. Oswald Sanders's *Spiritual Leadership*. I was amazed to see how much good leadership involves. A wide body of knowledge, a large set of skills, and a high quality of character are all required. The reading continued as I moved into other leadership positions, and I came to see increasingly clearly how important and complex leadership is. But as I continued to read about leadership there was one book I could not find: the book that put together the whole leadership life cycle from start to finish. I wanted a sense of where to begin, what comes next, and what happens after that, right through to the finish. I wanted the overall story into which every chapter of leadership fits, if such a book had been written.

---

1. I am grateful to John Guest for sharing this insight with me and for all the other ways he helped me grow as a leader.

After six years leading a church in West London, I moved with my family to Trinity School for Ministry in Pittsburgh, USA, to teach theology to students preparing for church leadership. I had visited Trinity on study leave after ten years in ordained ministry in London and found an unusual affinity with it, so I was delighted to have the chance to teach there when a vacancy arose. One of my colleagues there taught on Christian leadership and asked me to speak to his students about what I had learned as leader of St Helen's Church, North Kensington. It was a fascinating challenge. It made me think back over those fast-moving years and how to describe them for students in a way that would help them prepare for their own leadership roles. But it was surprisingly hard to do. On the one hand, it was a constant series of services and meetings, of emails and events, of praying and preaching, of succeeding and failing, and of slowly getting to grips with what I was supposed to be doing. It all seemed so haphazard. On the other hand, there was a sense of one season leading to another, and then to a third, and so on, until it was time to leave. There were signs of distinctive stages in that rich and exciting time. I was asked to give the lecture again the following year, which gave me the chance to refine the ideas further. They were clarified even more when I gave the lecture a year later. As I continued to get greater insight into the material, and did other teaching on leadership in various contexts, fresh light began to dawn on the subject. I started to discern five major phases of leadership during those years at St Helen's Church. I then looked at the work of other leaders and saw the same pattern there. I discussed these phases with leaders I knew, including those who find themselves in second-chair leadership positions supporting an overall leader as I now do myself, and found they resonated there too. Perhaps this was the beginning of the book I had been wanting someone to write.

The Five Phases Of Leadership

The five phases of leadership that began to emerge from these reflections were:

- Establish trust
- Cultivate leaders
- Discern vision
- Implement plans
- Transition out

These are the stages of leadership that leaders typically pass through, and each one of them is crucial. Nothing significant can happen until trust has been established. Other leaders will need to be identified, equipped and deployed into various roles for the necessary range of activities to take place. A vision is needed to clarify what you are trying to achieve, together with a purpose statement saying why you want to bring it about, and core values expressing how you want people to do so. Plans then need to be drawn up to turn ideas into initiatives to see the vision realized. Finally, leaders need to know when they have finished, so that they can transition out well. Without trust, leadership is simply not possible; without other leaders, the scope of operation will be limited; without vision, it will be hard to provide a sense of direction; without plans, the vision is unlikely to come about; and without transitioning out in a properly considered way, some of the leader's good work will be lost. Every phase of leadership matters.

These five phases of leadership apply to all kinds of leaders: team captains, army commanders, band leaders, film producers, chief executives, prime ministers, tribal chiefs and presidents, but they are especially clearly seen in the leadership of the captain of a ship. A captain has to inspire trust in everyone on board so they can feel confident that the ship is in good hands. He or she must recruit a good crew, deploy them where they can serve best, and have the right leaders in place. The captain will also need to know where they are going and keep that destination in mind at all times. He or she will need to work on implementing plans for the journey by navigation, managing provisions, and meeting the challenges of any storms along the way. He or she must also know when they have arrived at port, so that everyone may disembark and the boat can be prepared for its next journey. The captain needs trust, leaders, vision, plans, and an awareness of arrival at the destination. That is the work of leadership.

The image of the captain of a ship, or indeed any of these other leaders, can help us see these stages of leadership unfold and clarify the role of a leader, assisting us to chart our own course, whether as the overall leader or as a leader in a supporting role. Farida Saïdi, undertook a study of church leadership in North Africa, and found that the metaphors most widely used by Christian leaders in that region, many of whom come from Muslim backgrounds, were chief or army chief, policeman, pope and king.[2] It is likely that, wherever we are leading, the prevailing culture will provide the primary leadership metaphors, since those tend to define leadership there. Whatever image we may think most suitable to our role, it is important that we see it redeemed for a Christian application, so that we do not inadvertently adopt the leadership styles of our

2. Farida Saïdi, *A Study of Current Leadership Styles in the North African Church* (Carlisle: Langham Monographs, 2013), 225.

local culture but instead that of our Christian commitments. Nor should we become too wedded to any one metaphor, since some situations may demand we operate with a different one. As Saïdi indicates, sometimes leadership roles require us to be more authoritarian or more democratic, sometimes more participative or more directive, sometimes more relational or more task orientated, and at other times more laissez-faire or more motivational.[3] We need to adapt our approach to our setting, and indeed to the maturity of those we lead,[4] if we are to lead people through a wide variety of circumstances.

These five phases seem to typically occur in the same order: establish trust, cultivate leaders, discern vision, implement plans, and transition out. Only once you have established trust, and raised up suitable leaders, can you discern vision together, and only then can you develop plans to make that vision a reality, and go on doing so until the time comes to leave. Occasionally, however, someone might arrive in a leadership position bringing a vision. So it was for Moses, who had been asked by God to take the Hebrew slaves out of captivity in Egypt on a journey to the promised land (Exod 3:7–10). He knew where he was taking the Israelites before he had become their leader. But he still had to establish trust, which took a while after a poor start when he killed an Egyptian slave driver (Exod 2:11–14), and the many ups and downs of the confrontations with Pharaoh (Exod 5–12). He also had to learn to cultivate leaders when his father-in-law, Jethro, impressed on him the need to share his leadership with others (Exod 18). And he needed to implement the plan to make the long and arduous journey to the land flowing with milk and honey, following God's leading by the pillar of cloud by day and the pillar of fire by night (Exod 13:21–22). There was also a transitioning out, albeit a rather ignominious one after he had disobeyed God and lost the privilege of leading his people into the land of Canaan (Deut 34:1–8). So the exact order of these phases may vary, but they typically seem to occur in the same sequence.

There is bound to be some overlap between these phases, since one may continue after the next has begun, which is why they are best called "phases" rather than "stages" of leadership. Establishing trust and cultivating leaders are ongoing tasks for any leader. Discerning vision may only need to be done occasionally, say every five or ten years, and then it may just be to confirm what is already in place. There also needs to be some implementation of plans before the vision is discerned as well as afterwards, since vision discernment

3. Saïdi, *Current Leadership Styles*, 26.

4. Walter C. Wright, *Relational Leadership: A Biblical Model for Leadership Service* (Carlisle: Paternoster, 2000), 39.

may take some time to come about. Transitioning out occurs only when the work is complete, but a leader should always be aware that this time will come so that, when it does, the organization is in good shape for the next leader to pick up where the previous one has left off, with minimal loss of momentum. So there is a sequence to these phases, but not a sense of one having to finish before the next one can begin. They also each have many different components, as we shall see. All five phases, however, are vital to the work of a leader, and having an overall sense of them should be helpful for anyone in leadership. They allow leaders to see the wood despite the trees.

The examples I use in the following chapters come primarily from the life of an English church and an American theological college, which might be called a seminary or Bible college in other contexts. They are included to help make these ideas more concrete. They do, however, have much wider application, for which readers may need to translate these examples into their own situation. To try to make this as easy as possible, I often use the phrase "church or organization" in the hope that the word "organization" will be applied broadly, not just to educational establishments, but also to homes, ministries, workplaces and any other kind of organization, great or small. I am also aware that I serve in the Anglican denomination, which has its own culture and terminology which are apparent from time to time, so I have included a glossary at the end. To further aid application to other situations and places, there are several examples provided from different contexts and countries.

This book is written to help leaders lead. You might just want to work through it on your own, using the "Taking It Further" exercises as you find helpful. Alternatively, you may wish to read it with a leadership mentor, which would enrich the experience significantly. It could prove a valuable study for small groups of leaders, perhaps bringing together people in similar roles. If you are part of a staff team, or you are a leader in a school, college or seminary, or have a broader oversight position like a bishop or an area superintendent, it could be used with your senior leadership team, with groups of pastors or with teams of employees. However you use it, I hope it will prove instructive in many ways that enable the mission of the church or organization to go forward powerfully.

With that overview in mind, let us look at each of the five phases of leadership.

Phase 1

Establish Trust

In the early 2000s, I was the vicar, or senior pastor, of St Helen's Church in North Kensington, West London. It was a time of many challenges and joys. I look back on it with deep gratitude, especially for the last three years when so many exciting things happened. But I also wonder if I would have been more fruitful and perhaps less anxious, especially in the first three years, if I had been aware of how leadership typically unfolds. For instance, when I arrived I could see a lot of things that needed urgent attention, and was aware of the danger of rushing to do them and making matters worse rather than better. But how long would it be before we could talk about rearranging the church furniture, changing the service times or moving people into other leadership roles? We had so much to sort out before we could even look at upgrading our dilapidated church hall, getting youth ministry going again or restarting a church plant. It was all very well to say that there are things you should not do when you start as a leader that would make complete sense later, but for how long would that initial slow progress go on? And what was the path that would take me from where I was to where I thought we needed to be?

That dilemma reminds me that when I was about ten years old I became concerned that if I and my whole generation continued growing at the same rate we had been growing until then and stopped around the age of sixteen, we would be much shorter than those who went before us. I had not learned about the teenage growth spurt. The rate of change truly can increase as time goes on. This is the kind of discovery you cannot work out by extrapolation. It comes from experience, ours and other people's. Leaders will want to know that change can occur more rapidly once trust has been established, and that may help them to be patient, and focus on building relationships.

As I looked back on my time at St Helen's Church from the vantage point of a theological college tutor, I gradually discerned that I had been through five major phases of leadership. I saw those same five phases again when I became principal, or president, of Trinity School for Ministry, and I am watching them repeat themselves as vice-principal, or vice-president, of Wycliffe Hall. They have been reinforced in numerous conversations with leaders of other institutions, and by reading the biographies of leaders. But the first and most essential phase for any leader is to establish trust. So let us begin by focusing our attention there.

Establish Trust: A Case Study

When I arrived at St Helen's Church, the congregation had been without an overall leader for nearly two years. It had been a major challenge to maintain the life of the church in all its complexity for such an unusually long time. Those in leadership roles felt the burden most acutely and were emotionally drained by it. When I arrived, I looked back over the attendance records and saw that in the first of those years, we had lost a third of the congregation. We had also lost a third of the giving. I didn't continue the calculation into the second year; it was too discouraging.

There were also a lot of problems to address. Some of them were very practical issues: the phone had stopped working, the sound system didn't function properly, and the electrical wiring was in poor shape. There was a memorable occasion during the evening of the institution service to launch my ministry at St Helen's Church, when someone turned on a light switch, and all the lights went out.

The church had other problems too. There had been a water leak that had resulted in a huge water bill. The Church Council was concerned about how to deal with it. Its two most senior members, the churchwardens, believed they were personally responsible for paying it, which they couldn't do. In addition, there was only one home group remaining; many of those in leadership were in their seventies and eighties; the Sunday services needed to be rethought to help them flow better; and the list could go on. These issues caused a lot of anxiety and distress. There was a great deal to do and I was new to the job. Where was I to begin?

The first thing we did was to get daily prayer meetings going for anyone who was available. We used the traditional Anglican services of Morning and Evening Prayer, whose value I had discovered in my previous role as curate, or assistant minister, of St John's Church, Hyde Park. There was a ready-made pattern of prayers and Bible readings that we could use, and the opportunity for spontaneous prayer during the intercessions. We offered up our work to God at the start of the day, and entrusted the challenges and needs of the church to the Lord at the end of it, leaving our burdens at the foot of the cross. It reminded us constantly that Christ is the head of the church, not us, and what we needed most was his daily direction and provision, and the empowerment of his Holy Spirit.

This is an indication that even before the vision-formation stage, the leader can make certain matters a priority. When Archbishop Justin Welby took office as leader of the Anglican Communion, he announced that his priorities would be the renewal of prayer and the religious life, reconciliation, and evangelism and witness. Those have clearly guided him in his leadership, as well as signalling to others where he wanted to invest his energies. Likewise, in any new leadership position it can be helpful to focus time on certain areas which are sure to improve the health of the church or organization. For me they were prayer, preaching and hospitality.

Then we began to renew our Sunday services. On Monday evenings, I would meet with the worship group leader; those who would announce hymns, read Scripture and lead the intercessions at the two morning services; the parish evangelist, who had a special concern for newcomers; and the pastoral care coordinator, who would update us on those in particular need. Of these, only the worship leader was paid. The others were volunteers. When Ian Dowsett joined the team as curate, or assistant minister, he came to the meetings too. We would review the services from the previous day and plan the services for the following Sunday. Both of these steps were very helpful. The review meant we could come back to any problems we had had in the Sunday services when we were in a position to resolve them and make changes for the future, rather than trying to deal with them during the busyness of the morning. The preview of the order of service for the following Sunday enabled us to improve our corporate worship. This part of the meeting began with a Bible study on the sermon text, which was enormously helpful for me as the preacher in terms of the interpretation, illustration and application of the Bible passage. We would then pray together for each other and for the church. Because we were getting together some of the most senior leaders, we were able to make more rapid changes to the services than I would even have dreamed of making on my own. And it meant I was getting to know these leaders, learning from them, and building trust.

I made preaching a high priority from the start, believing this is the primary work of ordained ministry, and that God uses it for good in innumerable ways. I would begin work on sermon preparation on Sunday afternoon, since we had no evening service, praying over the text and doing the translation and commentary work in search of the overall message and the main points, ready for the Monday evening meeting. By starting then, I would have most of the week to reflect on the passage, and to look out for illustrations and applications. On Wednesday morning I would write the sermon, normally in outline form. I prefer that format for preaching, but it also proved helpful later when more home groups started meeting. They could use the sermon notes for their study, together with some application questions that I added. Then on Saturday evening I would go over the sermon and make adjustments – sometimes quite major ones! – and try to get to know it in readiness to deliver it on Sunday morning. Occasionally I would rehearse the sermon in the pulpit since the church was just next door. I found that very helpful. That whole time of sermon preparation and being immersed in God's Word was enormously engaging and encouraging to me, reminding me of God's trustworthiness. It also proved a blessing to the congregations.

We were very intentional about hospitality, having many people over for meals, especially for Sunday lunch. In view of the small numbers we were dealing with, it was normally possible to offer this to anyone who visited the church. Depending on the situation, we might invite a visitor over on his or her first Sunday, since we always had sufficient for one or two extras, thanks to my wife, Cathy, and her gift of hospitality. This proved highly effective in helping newcomers feel connected to the church. There were also times when we wanted a longer conversation with church members, and being able to say we had spaces for lunch served us well. Otherwise, we might meet up during the week at a local coffee shop or restaurant. That had the additional advantage of making us more connected with nearby businesses and local people who might not have any particular connection to the church. Sometimes this led to pastoral and evangelistic conversations.

During the week, I made pastoral visits, got to know the neighbourhood, and attended meetings for the church and community. I worked my way through the practical problems that were causing so much distress. That involved making a lot of phone calls to individuals and companies that could help us. One of those calls that I remember fondly was to the borough council, which sent a representative to take a look at what had caused the water leak. They acknowledged that it had been caused by the root of one of their trees so they would pay for the damage it had done. What a relief!

Looking back, I can see that the first three or so years were largely a matter of establishing trust. I needed to be patient in getting to know the life of the church and attend to the many problems we had before we could start to think about a long-term vision, or how we could replant a church nearby, as our bishop, Michael Colclough, had asked us to do. The leader of a cathedral in South Carolina, USA, described a similar season in his leadership there, saying: "You can't start talking about the long-term future, or even vacation plans, with someone who is in intensive care!" That was a helpful image. And as we worked on these problems, and saw some encouraging early victories, we witnessed the level of distress go down, and the degree of trust go up.

Starting a leadership role by needing to deal with such practical issues is by no means unique to me. When I was teaching these principles at the Anglican Leadership Institute in South Carolina, USA, I met Francis Barongo. He serves in the Bunyoro-Kitara Diocese of Uganda and had faced many such problems, but on a much larger scale. He arrived in his new position to find that his main church had doors that didn't lock, some toilets had missing door frames, there was no kitchen, and there was a shocking state of dirtiness everywhere. As archdeacon, he was responsible for the repair of the houses of other church leaders in the area too, and for securing motorcycles for them, among other things. Francis was delighted to tell me that seven of the eight congregation leaders had motorcycles by the time we met. That kind of attention to practical problems builds trust and establishes strong relationships for the future, when we can get to other priorities. For Francis, that chiefly meant being able to provide further training for church leaders.

Gradually, we moved beyond the initial stages of the turnaround period, and were able to start focusing more on our mission to the neighbourhood. The Diocese of London was training local churches in running missions, and Bishop Michael had invited St Helen's to take part. It was a great example of bishops leading the church in mission. I was already committed to treating baptism preparation, marriage preparation and funerals as opportunities for evangelism, and to seeing confirmation as commissioning for Christian ministry, but I had not thought of undertaking a mission quite so soon. However, it turned out that the timing was good. That mission, and the Alpha Course run as part of the follow-up, were a tonic for the church, helping people understand the Christian faith better and generating a lot of excitement. When the course came to an end, the discussion groups remained together as home groups under the same leadership, so they were established in advance of meeting in a home, which made the task of the group leader less daunting. It also meant that home groups were being built up again.

Many of the connections we made with the wider community came through renting out our church hall. It was an unusually large space in an area of London where there was a shortage of such facilities. But it was in poor condition and we did not have the money to improve it. It needed a lot more than a coat of paint. It required additional toilet facilities, a better kitchen, and much more besides. In fact, it had deteriorated to the point where some groups which had previously rented the hall were finding more attractive alternatives elsewhere. One of these losses had been especially painful for us. It meant losing an expected rental worth a third of our annual budget.

Not long after that, I was talking with the head teacher of a Montessori school that used the church hall for occasional events. She said that if it were in better shape, they would use the building more often. I started to ask questions and found out that the directors of the school had attended St Helen's Church as children. When I contacted them, it was clear they were very interested in the hall and willing to invest in it if they could have regular use of its facilities during school hours. In the end an agreement was reached. They put in three state-of-the-art classrooms with air conditioning – which is rare in London – a kitchen, new toilets, including one with disabled access, and a shower. They also upgraded the stage with a new sound system and stage lighting, and landscaped the garden. Not only did that provide a renewed hall that the church and community could use outside school hours, it also gave us a twenty-five-year rental agreement that stabilized our finances. In addition to all that, we had a much stronger connection with the school. What a transformation! What a lot for which to thank God!

As trust was growing and problems were being overcome, we also began to consider the church plant we had been asked to restart. St Francis Church and house had formerly been the responsibility of a neighbouring church which had established them, but they had been unable to sustain the congregation there, so the buildings were transferred to us for a replant. Both of them had fallen into a very poor state, with water running into the buildings and plants growing out of them! But they were at the centre of three social housing estates, and ideally situated for a church plant.

We decided to start by trying to get the house up to the standard where we could rent it out for Christian workers in the neighbourhood and for a youth worker for St Helen's. The hope was that it would eventually be suitable for an assistant minister to live in and lead the church plant. But work on St Francis house quickly ran over budget, despite the oversight of an architect. We faced an overspend equal in size to what we had recently lost in rental income! And we heard it in the same week we learned about that. It meant that we were facing a deficit of two-thirds of our annual budget! That was a very hard week. I felt an acute sense of failure. I feared it might undermine trust in my leadership, and that it could even turn the congregations against the church plant. Mercifully, I was quite established at this point, and no one blamed me for the overspend on the house, or for the loss of rental income. And the desire to see St Francis replanted was undimmed.

The restoration of the house was eventually completed and tenants were found for it. The losses were covered with help from a nearby church, which had a youth worker renting one of the rooms. Repairing the house meant we had closer links with those housing estates, and with the local ministries that were renting rooms in it, which included the Salvation Army. It also meant we had housing for a youth worker, so we could restart the youth work that had lapsed. Later that house became the home of Ian Dowsett, who, with his wife, Ruth, would lead the church plant. This again was a major cause for joy.

As I look back over those early years, I can see that every part of it involved establishing trust. Paying attention to the problems and getting them solved played a vital part in that, as did the time spent with the members of the church, especially its leadership. It also helped that I spent time with local people, such as those who used our church hall. Cathy also co-chaired a neighbourhood committee which worked with the borough council to bring about the renewal of the local park, which had become very run-down and a centre for antisocial activities. Out of those relationships good things came, in answer to our prayers.

How that trust is established will vary considerably according to our context. An Indian church planter discovered that he was not welcome if he simply arrived in a village and started to preach. So he took time to establish trust by giving guitar lessons to children. That gave him entry into the children's homes, where he would meet families and offer to pray for them in the name of Jesus. From that start, he established a church that has been able to reach out to the whole village. Evangelists in India have found that praying for people, especially for healing, protection, provision or deliverance, opens the door to faith before they can speak of Jesus as Saviour, then Jesus as Lord, and eventually Jesus as supreme God. Offering prayer for free is itself strikingly different from the animist priests, who charge to offer sacrifices for healing. In other areas of India, starting schools has been the way to establish trust. In one such case, a single school led to seven churches being planted within three years.[1] As American President Theodore Roosevelt memorably put it, "People don't care how much you know until they know how much you care." Wherever we start, we need to begin by building trust.

1. I am grateful to Dr Finny Philip, Principal of Filadelfia Bible College, Udaipur, India, for these stories.

I found those early years very challenging, and faced strong opposition from some members of the church for several of the changes we made. I was enormously glad of the support from my bishop and others in the diocese, from local ministers of my own denomination and others, from leaders in the church, and from others who helped me along the way. I met with many individuals and groups to talk about what we were doing, including my mentor, David Prior, and they would share ideas with me and pray. I was also grateful to be working on a PhD at the time, and the faculty and students of King's College, London, where I was studying, were a great blessing. Cathy was a huge support. All these networks were an enormous help to me, especially in those difficult early years.

Establish Trust: The Ingredients

Every aspect of leadership involves trust, since leadership depends on influence, influence depends on relationships, and relationships depend on trust. Discovering what the current situation of the church or organization is involves trust, raising up leaders to join us in the work involves trust, discerning a vision for the future involves trust, and implementing plans to get there involves trust too. Trust is vital to all these things, and it generally takes a significant time to develop. If a leader is already known by those he or she will be leading, that is a great help, and gives the leader a head start. That was the case for me when I took over leadership of Trinity School for Ministry, having served on its faculty. But it was not the case for me when I arrived at St Helen's Church, and it is very common for leaders to have to build trust from scratch.

So what is needed for that trust to be established? How is the leader to become trustworthy? This is a big question for leaders at any level of responsibility, and it involves every aspect of Christian discipleship. One way to draw out the main ingredients for building trust is to look at that great description of mature Christian character, the fruit of the Spirit: "But the fruit of the Spirit is love, joy, peace, patience, kindness, goodness, faithfulness, gentleness, self-control; against such things there is no law" (Gal 5:22–23, ESV). These are the qualities that, taken together, make someone trustworthy.

This is, of course, not to suggest that only Christians are trustworthy, or that the Holy Spirit is the only means of becoming more trustworthy. The Bible tells us that everyone is made in the image of God (Gen 1:27) and to some extent mirrors godly qualities like those described in the fruit of the Spirit. Also, all people can train themselves to be more trustworthy by seeking out the wisdom of others and learning from their mistakes. What we are offering here has two parts. The first is a description of the qualities that undergird trustworthy people, reflecting godly characteristics to which all may aspire, and that make for good leaders. The second is an explanation of the way Christians see the presence of the Holy Spirit in their lives animating and developing those qualities. It is a reminder that Christianity is not primarily about keeping rules and trying to please God, but about a relationship with God as our heavenly Father, which means that we have the Spirit of God at work in our lives to make us more like Jesus. My aim here is to show how this work of the Holy Spirit can make us more trustworthy.

The character formation that leads to trustworthy Christian leaders is primarily the work of the Holy Spirit, and it is crucial not to forget that. We do have important obligations to hear the Word of God and seek to live by it with the support of the people of God, but we need the Holy Spirit to do the heavy lifting of character development. When we moved to Pittsburgh, we bought a house with a garden. The previous owners sold us their lawnmower. It was a rusty, old motor mower, but it still cut the grass. Mowing the lawn was very hard work. I would come in exhausted afterwards, although we did not have much grass to cut. By the third year of this struggle, I was wondering if we needed a new mower. I was out mowing the lawn again soon afterwards and looked at the lever on the side of the mower handle. I had tried pulling it before but without success. With little to lose, I pulled that lever until it moved. When it did, the front wheels suddenly engaged and began to turn on their own. I could simply follow behind the mower, steering it as necessary, and get the lawn mown. What a transformation! In a similar way, human beings are created to rely on the inner working of the Holy Spirit to animate us and enable us to live fruitful lives. There is still work for us to do, but it is to be done by the power of the Spirit.

So let us keep that in mind as we consider each aspect of the fruit of the Spirit and see how it is related to the trustworthiness of a leader.

Love

The Christian leader should be motivated by love, inspired by the love of God revealed in Christ crucified, and empowered by the Spirit of love at work in our lives. We are called to love the Lord our God, and to love other people as ourselves (Mark 12:30–31). This immediately takes the focus off the leader and puts it onto the led. As apologist Amy Orr-Ewing puts it, "Christian leadership should never be about ourselves. It is ultimately focused on a purpose that is larger and wider than individual ambition, because it seeks God's kingdom coming on earth."[2] So it means fostering only the kind of ambition that is focused on God's glory, rather than selfish ambition or self-glorification (Phil 2:3).

Jesus called his disciples to this self-sacrificing love when he told them to wash each other's feet and to lay down their lives for their friends (John 13:14; 15:13). This love will therefore be manifested in *serving others*, not seeing how they can serve us, following the example of Jesus (Mark 10:45). As King Solomon's advisers wisely counselled his son Rehoboam, "If you will be a servant to this people today and serve them, and speak good words to them when you answer them, then they will be your servants for ever" (1 Kgs 12:7). This requires listening to people and getting to know them and their family, their history and their world. It means remembering names and being aware of what is going on in their lives, at home and at work. That might involve keeping a notebook of those things in the early days, but this will help build trust in you as a leader. It is also vital to the ministries of preaching and teaching if you have them. It will play a central role too in helping you to lead people into God's purposes, which, as leadership experts Henry and Richard Blackaby point out, is the goal of Christian leadership.[3] So the priority of love in the character of a Christian leader is a call to servant leadership, a concept which has gained wide currency in leadership theory as a result of the work of Robert Greenleaf.[4]

This love will also mean wanting to learn all you can about the history of the church or organization and about its neighbourhood, in order to understand them better and discern what is currently going on. This is part of what leadership scholars call "sense-making," that vital role of understanding the issues you will need to address. That knowledge is to lead primarily to prayer, sometimes with people, and often for them. I have found it helpful to have a list for my daily private prayers so I do not forget those needs. How powerful it is to be able to say to someone, "I am praying for you every day." It is a simple but meaningful expression of love. And the more we listen and pray, the more we love. So love is not primarily a matter of feelings, but of service. And that love lies at the core of being trustworthy, and makes for a leader whom people want to follow.

---

2. Quoted in Michael Green, *Radical Leadership in the New Testament and Today* (London: SPCK, 2017), 101.

3. Henry and Richard Blackaby, *Spiritual Leadership*, rev. ed. (Nashville: Broadman & Holman, 2011), xiv.

4. He first presented the theory in a 1970 essay "The Servant as Leader," which was substantially revised in 1973 and published by Cambridge, MA: Center for Applied Studies.

Joy

Another characteristic of the fruit of the Spirit is joy. We have the privilege of following a risen saviour who is ruler over all things. We know that even death itself is not the end, and that "no eye has seen, nor ear heard, nor the human heart conceived, what God has prepared for those who love him" (1 Cor 2:9). The challenges of leadership need not weigh us down nor overwhelm us if we hold onto these great truths. There can be joy in our lives even in the times of greatest difficulty, when worldly happiness might be in short supply. As the apostle Paul says, we are to "rejoice in the Lord always; again I will say, rejoice" (Phil 4:4). In 2019 Michael Green, a great Christian leader and evangelist who had ministered all around the world, went to be with his Lord. He was based at Wycliffe Hall for the last season of his ministry, so I had the privilege of spending time with him there. He is greatly missed for many reasons, but what I miss most is the infectious joy that he spread everywhere he went. That joy is one of the gifts leaders bring to their ministry, by the Holy Spirit. We have a quiet confidence about a brighter future, and that too helps breed trust.

Such joy means that we can *praise and worship God*, and lead others in that praise and worship, in all the seasons of life. We can cultivate joy by counting our blessings every day, deliberately focusing our attention on God's goodness, on answered prayers, and on those things that bring a smile to our faces. My daily prayer list includes a section on thanksgiving for answered prayer to try to stimulate this joyful attitude. Drawing attention to God's blessings and praising people for work well done are great motivators for living the Christian life, and grow trust not just in us as leaders but also in God and God's faithfulness. We should regularly step back from the current problems and spend time thanking God for every good gift and cultivating an attitude of thankfulness (Eph 5:20). This helps people maintain a positive outlook, like bubbles of buoyant air helping keep us afloat. May it be said of us as it was of American evangelist Dwight L. Moody, "One could not be downhearted or defeated in his presence."[5] Cultivating such joy also means we can laugh. It enables us to remain positive in challenging environments, which has all sorts of benefits for effectiveness and relationships, as Dr Martin Seligman shows in his book *Learned Optimism*.[6] So may the Lord grant us that Spirit-inspired joy that makes us a source of joy, and helps us be better and more trustworthy leaders.

5. Quoted by Blackaby, *Spiritual Leadership*, 362.

6. Martin Seligman, *Learned Optimism* (Boston: Nicholas Brearley, 2018).

Peace

With that love and joy comes peace, a peace that passes all understanding (Phil 4:7). It is a peace that means well-being and harmony, and stands in contrast with works of the flesh such as enmity, strife, rivalry, dissensions and divisions (Gal 5:20). This peace is rooted in the ascension of Jesus Christ, who always lives to make intercession for us (Heb 7:25) and is present with us by the Holy Spirit (Eph 4:3). Our leadership is always under Christ's leadership since he is the head of the church (Col 1:18) and he is Lord of all (Matt 28:18). He is praying for us and guiding us through his Word and by his Spirit. So it is not all up to us! Our task is to be faithful to Christ's call and to do what he calls us to do, even if that does not register as worldly success. Our responsibility is to seek the Lord's will and to strive to be someone "after [God's] heart," as King David was (Acts 13:22). That way the glory goes to God, where it belongs, rather than puffing leaders up with pride, which can lead to a fall (Prov 16:18).

This peace helps leaders not to become paralysed by *anxiety* and fear but to learn to acknowledge those anxieties and hand them over to the Lord, because God cares for us (1 Pet 5:7). In the words of Joseph Medlicott Scriven's gospel hymn, "O what peace we often forfeit, / O what needless pain we bear, / All because we do not carry / everything to God in prayer."[7] In this way we can learn to be what family systems theorists such as Edwin Friedman call a "non-anxious presence"[8] – in other words, people who bring a sense of calm to anxious situations and help others get through them. No one wants to be on board a plane with a pilot who panics when they are flying through turbulence. We want a calm and reassuring voice that lets us know that there is no need for alarm, unless there truly is a crisis for which we need to prepare. As management researchers have seen, the mood of leaders affects those they lead through what they call "mood contagion."[9] When we can be at peace even in a storm, it helps others think calmly and clearly, and not react impulsively. That peace is a great gift of God to the church and therefore to the world, and this too builds trustworthiness.

---

7. Joseph Medlicott Scriven, "What a Friend We Have in Jesus" (1855).

8. Edwin H. Friedman, *A Failure of Nerve: Leadership in the Age of the Quick Fix* (New York: Seabury, 1997).

9. Daniel Goleman, Richard Boyatzis and Annie McKee, "Primal Leadership," in Harvard Business Review, *HBR's 10 Must Reads On Emotional Intelligence* (Boston: Harvard Business Review Press, 2015), 25.

Patience

A fourth characteristic is patience, which is another vital quality of Spirit-filled leaders, and one that often only develops over time. Patience is an aspect of love, for "love is patient" (1 Cor 13:4). It is about giving the gift of time to others and to ourselves. It takes time for a leader to become established, it takes time for others to emerge as leaders, and it takes time to get to know which changes would be improvements, and how to bring those changes about. It also takes time for us to become the leaders God wants us to be. So, whether we like it or not – and I have to admit I don't like it – we need to be patient. In fact, by pushing too hard or too soon, we may only increase the resistance to change both now and in the future, like trying to force open an automatic door. While sometimes immediate change may be necessary, it is generally wise to avoid making significant changes for the first year or so in any new leadership position.

Allowing time to get to know why things are the way they are is an act of love and respect, and may help us avoid making changes that we will later regret and perhaps even find ourselves in the uncomfortable position of having to reverse. It shows a degree of trust in other people who have made those decisions and may still be around, and that trust might then be reciprocated. Remember that as we become more established, change may occur more quickly. Leaders simply have to live with uncertainty, and must sometimes wait to see things resolve. You may need to deliberately slow yourself down by doing other things, perhaps by spending more time building relationships inside and outside the church or organization, continuing your studies as I did, or working on other initiatives within and beyond the organization you lead, to allow things to develop at God's own pace. We need to remember the old adage "more haste, less speed," and learn to work on God's timescale. That too will make us better leaders.

Kindness

Kindness is also required in a leader. This too is an aspect of love, since "love is kind" (1 Cor 13:4). It is a matter of giving good gifts to others as our Father in heaven gives good gifts to us (Matt 7:11; Jas 1:17). This will involve constantly asking, "What would be good for this person, this ministry, this church, or this organization?" So kindness is not a matter of saying "yes" to every request, as some might imagine. In fact, it will often mean saying "no" or "not yet," which will frequently be a hard message to deliver. It helps if we remember that God's kindness is intended to lead us to repentance (Rom 2:4), which is fundamental to restoring our relationship with God and empowering us with the gift of the Holy Spirit. And our kindness should play a vital role in putting us in good relationship with those we lead. It includes being willing to forgive those who offend us, and developing the necessary toughness to keep on being kind and remain in leadership for the long run. Bishop Festo Kivengere, who played a huge role in the revival in south-western Uganda, had to flee for his life in 1973 after speaking out against President Idi Amin's tyrannical behaviour. He went on to write a book with the striking title *I Love Idi Amin*. He didn't just preach a gospel of forgiveness, he lived it out in a way that allowed him to help with the rebuilding of the nation after Amin's downfall. That is a remarkable example of kind leadership.

The kindness that gives only good gifts, not necessarily what people want, takes *courage*, which is the willingness to do what we believe to be right even though we expect to face difficulties for doing it. Courage is indispensable for any leader. It is essential if you are to remain on target as an organization when pressures mount to change direction, and if you are to stay the course when major challenges come your way. Often this courageous kindness is first learned from our parents or carers who may show us something of God's parental love in sometimes saying to us "no" and "not yet." As adults our homes can also be places where we go on learning courageous kindness from those with whom we share our lives most intimately. Courage should also develop from how we treat our friends, where we are willing to speak truthfully to each other and hear the truth from each other even when that may not be what we want to hear. Jesus called his disciples "friends" (John 15:15), and that is a healthy goal for Christian leaders, provided we don't show favouritism. "A managerial myth says we can't be too close to our associates. We can't be friends with people at work. Well," say leadership researchers James Kouzes and Barry Posner, "set this myth aside."[10] We should be cultivating this kindness wherever we can: at home, among friendship groups, and at work. So it is good to hear again what God said to Joshua: "Be strong and courageous; do not be frightened or dismayed, for the LORD your God is with you wherever you go" (Josh 1:9). Such courageous kindness is another key to the trust-growing and relationship-building that lie at the heart of the leader's work.

---

10. Quoted in Blackaby, *Spiritual Leadership*, 359.

Goodness

Leaders are also to exhibit goodness, a word often related in the New Testament to *generosity*. This is the call to holiness of life, a life which increasingly reflects the holiness of God (Lev 11:44). It is what the German Reformer Martin Luther called the second kind of righteousness: sanctification, when we are being made righteous, which follows the first kind of righteousness: justification, when we are declared righteous through receiving the forgiveness of sins. This is the goodness that God grows in us in addition to that which God grants to us. Church of Scotland minister Robert Murray M'Cheyne famously said, "The greatest need of my people is my personal holiness." This is a demanding call that could easily cause us to feel deflated, but it can instead be heard positively as an invitation to take seriously the call to sanctification, as God's Spirit is at work in us "both to will and to work for his good pleasure" (Phil 2:13). It is about a fundamental determination to do the right thing in the right way and for the right reasons. It is about doing what we believe will please God, rather than seeking to please ourselves or other people. An accountability group or soul friend can be a great assistance in living such a life. It is important to stay close to the Lord in prayer, Bible reading and fellowship, to be quick to repent when we fall into sin, and to ask to be filled with the Holy Spirit daily for the demanding but wonderful work of leadership.

Every time we open ourselves to God for the continuing work of reform and renewal in our lives will prove to be a blessing not only to us but also to the people we lead. One of my faculty colleagues at Trinity tells the story of driving home during a period of staff conflict in the church where he was a leader. He saw someone struggling with a flat tyre. Initially he drove on, thinking he had more important things to do, but he felt convicted and went back to help. The driver turned out to be the relative of a prominent member of the church, and his stopping to assist had a profound effect on her and others in the congregation. These experiences may be difficult at the time, but they often lead to a new generous goodness, giving of our time and resources sacrificially for the Lord and for kingdom work, as we grow in our trust in God's provision for all our needs. That generosity, alongside integrity and humility, stands as a vital characteristic of leaders, as Rick Warren observes reflecting on the work of management consultant Peter Drucker.[11] This is a reminder that these qualities are of interest not just to Christians; they are of value to every leader.

11. Rick Warren on Peter Drucker and the Characteristics of Great Leaders, in a speech honouring what would have been Drucker's one hundredth birthday. Published by the Drucker Institute on https://www.youtube.com/watch?v=iPH8VpI-H7I, accessed 13 November 2020.

Faithfulness

Faithfulness in a leader is central to establishing trust. It is first about a steady faith in God, and God's Word and promises, and second about faithfulness to our word and promises. As leaders we are rightly held to higher standards in these things because of the responsibilities we carry. We need to be people who let our "'yes' be yes and [our] 'no' be no" (Jas 5:12). In their research into leadership, Kouzes and Posner found that the key thing for establishing trust was that the leader did what the leader said he or she would do.[12] We need to be careful not to take the easy way out by breaking a "minor commitment" or by telling the "small lie." Clearly, we need to speak with sensitivity and graciousness, but we need to be people of the truth who have no fear of something we say being later exposed as deceit. As Jesus said, "Whoever is faithful in a very little is faithful also in much; and whoever is dishonest in a very little is dishonest also in much" (Luke 16:10).

Good *communication* is vital for developing a reputation for faithfulness, with honest, open and transparent sharing of the joys and challenges of the church or organization. When things are going badly, people tend to assume they are even worse than they are unless you share the difficulties frankly. We saw this at work at Trinity School for Ministry when we faced three significant challenges at once: a great recession, a major realignment within the main denomination we served, and a leadership transition, since I had just arrived in post. Open sharing and inviting prayer, wisdom and support made all the difference to us. The appropriate sharing of your own vulnerabilities can also be helpful in building trust,[13] though over-sharing should be avoided, or it may come back to haunt you. When you make mistakes, it is vital to admit them quickly, keeping your supervisor informed as necessary. Take responsibility for your shortcomings, ask for forgiveness, make reparation where possible, learn from your mistakes, and then move on. All this will help you build a reputation for being a person of integrity.

Gentleness

Gentleness is about the way we exercise power. It means not being overbearing, like pagan leadership (Matt 20:25), but instead keeping our strength under

12. James Kouzes and Barry Posner, *The Leadership Challenge: How to Make Extraordinary Things Happen in Organizations*, 5th ed. (San Francisco: Wiley, 2012), 39.

13. See Rob Goffee and Gareth Jones, *Why Should Anyone Be Led by You? What It Takes to Be an Authentic Leader* (Boston: Harvard Business Review Press, 2019), 62.

control. This stands in sharp contrast to the harsh works of the flesh, such as fits of anger (Gal 5:20). Leaders do not need to shout or intimidate, but should express themselves in a gentle voice and with a light touch. A gentle leader is ready to let others get the credit for success but to take the blame him- or herself when things go wrong. Such gentleness can be misunderstood as weakness where more aggressive leadership is held in high esteem. But as Moses saw when his meek leadership was challenged by Aaron and Miriam, it is for God to defend the leaders of the people of God (Num 12:1–16). Gentleness also means avoiding sending quick emails, or messages and letters while we are feeling upset. Gentle leaders remember that it is one thing to know what needs to be said, and another to know how best to say it. Canadian entrepreneurial leader Peter Legge draws attention to the power of tact, and how valuable it is for building strong relationships.[14] The apostle Paul tells the church in Philippi, "let your gentleness be known to everyone" (Phil 4:5), and instructs Timothy to seek gentleness in those he recognizes for leadership (1 Tim 3:3). So it may come as no surprise that when a retired bishop wanted to give one piece of advice to a former chaplain as he was about to be consecrated bishop, he said, "The most important thing for a bishop is to increase [in] gentleness."[15]

This gentleness is a sign of *humility*, the quality that Christ demonstrates in his willingness to wash his disciples' feet (John 13:3–12) and that he commends in his followers (John 13:14). It is seen in cleaning dishes and taking out the rubbish. Paul emphasizes this humility when he says, "Do nothing from selfish ambition or conceit, but in humility regard others as better than yourselves" (Phil 2:3). Such humble gentleness is very winsome, and we know that God opposes the proud but lifts up the humble (Matt 23:12). However, it is notoriously hard to cultivate. Archbishop William Temple once remarked, "Humility does not begin with the giving of service; it begins with the readiness to receive it. For there can be much pride and condescension in our giving of service."[16] Humility grows through making prayer a priority, by noticing the ways in which God provides all that is needed, and by a willingness to take the places of lowliness. That humility is a vital asset for any leader.[17] Alongside fierce resolve, it has been identified as a characteristic of the highest level of

14. Peter Legge, *The Power of Tact 2.0* (Burnaby, British Columbia: Eaglet, 2018).

15. Bishop William Greer to Bishop Richard Hare, quoted in Steven Croft, *The Gift of Leadership – According to the Scriptures* (Norwich: Canterbury Press, 2016), 54.

16. William Temple, *Readings in John's Gospel* (New York: Morehouse, 1985), 203.

17. As Harvard management professor Clayton M. Christensen explains in "How Will You Measure Your Life?," Harvard Business Review, *HBR's 10 Must Reads on Managing Yourself* (Boston: Harvard Business Review Press, 2010), 11.

leadership in Jim Collins's seminal book on leadership, *Good to Great*.[18] So let us cultivate and celebrate that humble gentleness that makes for trustworthy and effective leaders.

Self-Control

Lastly, establishing trust relies on self-control. Rather than being led by our personal desires, we are called upon to be led by the Holy Spirit, and to have our will increasingly brought into alignment with God's will for our lives. This too stands in stark contrast to the works of the flesh, which include sexual immorality, envy, idolatry (which is equated with greed in Col 3:5) and drunkenness (Gal 5:19). All of these quench the work of the Holy Spirit in our lives. They are also temptations through which many leaders have fallen. This is a call to self-discipline which is essential for the follow-through needed in every aspect of leadership. Such self-control is not much praised in contemporary secular society, where the emphasis is on free self-expression and being true to our feelings and dreams. But leaders cannot expect to achieve much just by following their feelings.

Leaders also experience greater challenges because of the demands of their work. This means that areas of weakness in our lives tend to be magnified under the pressures of leadership. If you are short-tempered without the responsibility of leadership, how much more so with it! And if you are married and your marriage is under strain without the pressures of leadership, how much more so with them! Let us attend to those areas in our lives that might end up undermining trust, and get help from those who can assist us. This call to self-control is a high and hard calling, but it is an invitation to live the Christian life to the full, by the power of the Holy Spirit. It is a call to lead by example.

By the enabling power of the Holy Spirit, leaders need to learn to manage their relationships, their money, their time, indeed their whole lives. Managing our *emotions* is perhaps one of the most challenging aspects of leadership. People notice when we are happy or sad, afraid or angry. They will be inclined to react to those emotions, often by mirroring what they see, and developing the mood contagion we noted earlier. That way, feelings can get quickly amplified, with anger breeding anger, and fear generating alarm. Learning to be aware of our emotions and taking steps to ensure they receive the appropriate attention is the best way to make sure they do not drive an organization in unhelpful directions. When we are angry, we need to take time to process what is making

18. Jim Collins, *Good to Great* (New York: HarperCollins, 2001), chapter 2.

us angry, perhaps by taking exercise, playing music, journaling, or talking about it with others. Then, once we are feeling calm, we can decide if anything must be done about it. Anger can give us an inflated sense of the justice of our position that raises our confidence as if we are ascending in a lift. The best thing to do is to stay in the lift and not to get out at the top and erupt like a volcano, but ride it all the way down to the ground before acting. The ability to manage such emotions plays a surprisingly large part in determining the level of leadership to which anyone can aspire, since more senior positions apply greater pressures and stir up stronger emotions. To use Zig Ziglar's adage, "attitude determines altitude." We may not have much say over what we feel, but we do have considerable say over how we respond to those feelings. Self-control makes all the difference here, and plays a major part in building trust.

The degree to which we can develop these trustworthy traits, and the rate at which they might emerge, will depend on our own experience of trust, especially in our formative years. Leadership scholar Simon Walker explains that if our main caregivers when we were growing up were too affirming, we can become over-confident (what he calls "shapers"); if they were conditional in their love, we become intensely dutiful ("definers"); if they appeared fragile, we can become too eager to please ("adaptors"); and if they were unreliable, we are likely to become unduly wary ("defenders").[19] To some extent, we may all experience one or more of these challenges because none of us had perfect parents, carers or role models as we grew up. Walker says the goal for leaders is to become free, by not being controlled by their need to rescue people, to succeed, to please, or to control. If we know ourselves to be the children of God, and that our true value comes from our Father in heaven whose love is perfect and unconditional, we can be delivered from the need to succeed at all costs.[20] Such insights can help leaders to understand themselves and others better, and enable us to address our own challenges, so that we can grow into more trustworthy leaders.

---

19. Simon P. Walker, *Leading out of Who You Are: Discovering the Secret of Undefended Leadership* (Carlisle: Piquant, 2007), especially 54–111.

20. Walker, *Leading Out of Who You Are*, 151–160.

Conclusion

Establishing trust is the first and foremost task of the leader. Peter Drucker goes so far as to say, "Leadership is an achievement of trust."[21] If we think it is all up to us to generate such trust, we may become discouraged. But it is the fruit of the Spirit that is revealed in all the components of a trustworthy leader, so we should have hope. That is why it matters so much that the Christian leader seeks to be filled with God's Holy Spirit every day (Eph 5:18). This is vital if we are to follow the direction of Jesus Christ on our leadership journeys.

The character described in the fruit of the Spirit is truly beautiful. Who wouldn't want to be led by someone like that? But it is not formed in a day or even fully formed in a lifetime. There is no shortcut to becoming trustworthy. It takes years of daily discipleship to produce the reputation for integrity that every leader needs. It can begin as a young child and continue to develop through all the seasons of life. Experiences of leadership can help accelerate some of this transformation, as can further study, especially in places such as theological colleges or seminaries, since they provide a greenhouse environment for leadership development, as I have the privilege of seeing every day. Apprenticeships in assistant leadership roles can also accelerate that growth, and then it needs to continue through the ongoing process of lifelong learning and character formation. Throughout all this, we want to continue to grow in trustworthiness, and learn to lead ourselves in a Christlike way so that we can do the same for others.

It was Stephen Neill, who served as bishop of Tirunelveli, India, who first drew my attention to the value of the fruit of the Spirit for describing Christian maturity in his book *The Christian Character.* He recognizes that these characteristics cannot be developed by some act of self-will. They really are the work of God. "The growth of our bodies took place without our even noticing it was happening until suddenly we realised we could see over the wall that a few months before had been too high for us. It is the same with the growth of our spirits – *if* we remain rooted in Christ and learn to grow as the trees and flowers do."[22] Our task is to stay close to Christ, and the Spirit will do the rest.

---

21. Peter F. Drucker, "Executive Summary: A Conversation with Peter Drucker on Leadership and Organizational Development." 5 February 2002, as edited by Joseph A. Maciariello, p. 5. Available at https://www.porchlightbooks.com/blog/excerpts/a-year-with-peter-drucker, accessed 13 November 2020.

22. Neill, *Christian Character*, 92.

Trust takes a long time to build, but very little time to lose. One lie, one fraudulent act, one inappropriate relationship is all it takes to undo a reputation established over many years. Even if no one finds out about it, such behaviour can be a cancer, undermining character which might lead to other failures. These things must be repented of and help found where necessary. Rebuilding trust takes even longer than building it in the first place. But without that trust, leadership is severely hampered, if it is possible at all. It stands at the heart of the leader's work, which is why godly character matters so much for the leader. It is the private work on our character that goes on back-of-stage which enables us to do the public work of leadership front-of-stage.[23] Lesslie Newbigin, who served for nearly forty years as a missionary in India, sets out the challenge plainly: "The minister's leadership of the congregation in its mission to the world will be first and foremost in the area of his or her own discipleship, in that life of prayer and daily consecration which remains hidden from the world but which is the place where the essential battles are either won or lost."[24]

Christian leaders face all the challenges confronting all leaders in our societies, but with the additional demands of being officers in a spiritual battle. We need God's presence to guide our feet every step of the way, and God's protection every day to "deliver us from evil" (Matt 6:13, ESV). So it is a matter of living under God's Word, in the power of the Holy Spirit, in the fellowship of the church, with godly mentors who can help us rise to this wonderful call to lead. We need to be

> like a tree planted by water,
> sending out its roots by the stream.
> It shall not fear when heat comes,
> and its leaves shall stay green;
> in the year of drought it is not anxious,
> and it does not cease to bear fruit.
> (Jer 17:8)

That will foster the trustworthy character on which all leadership depends.

Taking It Further

How might you grow as a leader in establishing trust?

1. Are you developing a reputation for being trustworthy?

23. See Walker, *Leading out of Who You Are*, chapter 3.
24. Lesslie Newbigin, *The Gospel in a Pluralist Society* (London: SPCK, 1989), 240–241.

2. What steps could you take to grow as a disciple of Jesus Christ, and who might help you with them?

3. Do you have character issues that need to be addressed so that trust in you is not undermined?

4. Who might be willing to serve as a mentor to help you grow as a leader?

5. Do you have a network of support and accountability around you, or could you develop one?

6. Is it time to see if there are new areas of leadership for you to explore?

7. What further reading or study of leadership might you undertake?

Phase 2

Cultivate Leaders

Developing trust never ends. Leaders need to continue building trust throughout their lives. However, trustworthiness alone is not enough. A leader will want to find other leaders, or potential leaders, to expand his or her sphere of influence and accomplish their mission. One of the major lessons I learned from my studies in preparation for ordained ministry was how much energy Jesus invested in his twelve disciples. Robert Coleman explains it well in his book *The Master Plan of Evangelism.*[1] With so many millions of people to reach, Jesus devoted a great deal of time to those twelve followers. He was preparing them for their work as apostles, the first leaders of the church, who would in turn find other leaders to preach, teach and lead the church in its worldwide mission. It was a ministry of multiplication.

If we are to make good use of the gifts God has given us, and the gifts God has given to others, we will want to identify and develop other leaders. This can play a major part in moving a church or organization from maintenance to mission. If you try to do all the leadership yourself, you will be hard pressed to expand beyond about seventy people – at least, that is what has been found among church leaders.[2] You will probably become exhausted by the demands of the work, as Moses did (Exod 18:18). However, with a team of leaders around you, and perhaps a team of leaders around each of them, the possibility for extension of the mission is limitless. Like Timothy, we need to pass on what we have been taught to the next generation and equip them for leadership (2 Tim 2:2). This means that we can train up many men and women to lead

1. Robert Coleman, *The Master Plan of Evangelism*, 2nd ed. (Ada, MI: Revell, 2010).

2. See discussions of church size theory. For instance, there is a helpful summary in "Overview of Church Size Theory: Size Types and Their Characteristics" (Episcopal Church Foundation, 2012), accessed 23 March 2020, https://www.ecfvp.org/uploads/tools/files/Overview_of_Church_Size_Theory1.pdf.

God's people in God's mission to the world. It is a reminder too that the leader's task is not to answer all the questions that might arise, or to have all the clever ideas that might be needed. It is, instead, to recognize good ideas when he or she sees them, to know when to implement them, and to give credit to the person who had them, who might well be another leader. And it is the overall leader's task to set up an organizational structure, with the right leaders in the right places, to enable the work to get done.

Cultivate Leaders: A Case Study

At St Helen's Church, there was a pressing need to identify new leaders from the start since we had so few younger leaders. What would happen when some of the seasoned leaders stepped down from their responsibilities? Where was the pipeline for new leaders? Cultivating the present and future leaders of the church was a major task and proved to be highly significant. It largely took place through four groups of people: the Church Council, the Ministry Leadership Team, ministry leaders, and the staff team.

The Church Council

First, we had the Church Council, which was responsible for assisting me in the overall running of the church and for the fulfilment of several legal obligations. We worked hard to provide clarity about the expectations for those who served in this way, especially in the run-up to elections. They should be committed disciples of the Lord Jesus who had gifts they could bring and skills they could offer. When we met as a council, we always had a time of Bible study and prayer so they did not become purely business meetings. This was to be a gathering of the senior spiritual leaders of the congregation.

When I arrived at St Helen's Church, I followed wise advice to make the first gathering of the council a social event. Cathy and I had them to our home for dinner. It allowed the council members to see the work that the diocese had done on our house, which had turned it from being rather unsuitable for its role into a delightful home, well designed for such hospitality. That was a great encouragement to everybody. It also meant we were able to connect in a more personal way and to relate not just as a group but also as individuals. There were some frank conversations that evening about how hard the previous two years had been, and how many challenges lay ahead. But having those issues emerge during the course of a dinner party helped people express their thoughts openly, and set the context for the council meetings that lay ahead.

I was always looking for opportunities for conversations with members of the council because I wanted to spend time mentoring them in their roles and to help them identify and mentor other leaders. I asked them what they thought were the issues of the day and what ideas they had for the future. Those conversations took place over coffee after church, when we met in the street or over meals at our home. They were precious times and played a major part in my orientation, and in cultivating leaders in the congregation.

The Ministry Leadership Team

The second group of leaders was the Ministry Leadership Team, which was formed towards the end of my time at St Helen's as part of an initiative by the Diocese of London. This brought together the ordained leadership, the churchwardens (two senior leaders elected by the church to work closely with me), the parish evangelist, the pastoral care coordinator, the worship group leader, the children's worker and the youth minister. This team came under the authority of the Church Council, and had oversight of the other groups of the church, providing a way to coordinate all these teams and individuals. We would gather once a month to look at the whole mission of the church. There was an initial commitment to serving for three years, and we had an annual review with a leadership consultant.

The agenda of our meetings included the following:

1. Bible study and prayer
2. Newcomers: next steps for them
3. Children and youth: ministries for children and young people
4. Mission: the evangelism and social action of the church
5. Discipleship: home groups, service opportunities, leadership development, and training
6. Pastoral care: those in need, the housebound, the hospitalized, and funerals
7. Practicalities: follow-up actions, resources and communications required

This allowed us to see how well we were integrating newcomers into the church, and what might be the best way to disciple them. We would think about how to develop our leaders through having them move to different ministries and take on larger responsibilities. It was also a wonderful opportunity to spot leaders who should consider ordained ministry or overseas mission, and to offer them a chance to serve not only in the various ministries including teaching roles, but also to read the Bible in church, to lead intercessions and occasionally, under supervision, to preach. This was all very exciting to see.

Ministry Leaders

Third, there were the ministry leaders, who led the children's groups, the youth ministry, the home groups, the Good Companions Group for seniors, the flower arrangers, the worship band, the welcome team, the outreach ministry, the healing ministry, and the pastoral care team. These people were leading front-line ministries through which we sought to make disciples of Jesus Christ. Every one of them played a vital role in the life of the church, and I wanted to be sure they felt well supported by me. Where possible, I would meet with them regularly, every month or so, to see how they were doing and to support them in their work. At the very least, I would try to have a conversation when I saw them after a church service. This enabled me to offer discipling and coaching, and to help them address the opportunities and challenges they were facing.

When more home groups got started, I gathered the leaders three or four times a year for worship, teaching, prayer and encouragement. I invited each ministry group to become like a home group, which meant having some time of worship, welcoming newcomers to their ministry, studying the Bible, having time for fellowship, and serving those outside the group – in their case, through their ministry. One of my hopes for this arrangement was to provide additional support for these leaders by gathering them with other leaders for that additional opportunity for worship and teaching. In practice, however, many of the ministry leaders found they could not commit the time to it, which I came to accept.

The Staff Team

Lastly, we had the staff team. Initially, this was just the two churchwardens and me. Later, others joined the team, including an assistant minister and a part-time administrator. We met weekly to look at what needed to be done in the church in order to implement what had been decided by the Church Council and Ministry Leadership Team. We shared responsibilities for practical tasks such as doing repairs, painting rooms and pastoral visitation, each according to our gifting. This was a source of hope for me when I was concerned about the sheer amount of work that needed to be done. It also meant we could try to model the humility which we sought in all our leaders.

It soon became clear to me that I needed to pay close attention to the recruitment of senior leaders and members of staff. They needed to be people who had the respect of the congregation and the maturity to take on such a major leadership position in the church. I also tried to keep in touch with those who had previously served in similar ways once they stepped down, so that I continued to benefit from their insights.

These staff meetings were a particular help in handling any concerns and complaints that arose. I knew that I could not accept all criticism as being true, but, on the other hand, I couldn't reject it all as being false. How was I to discern the difference without being defensive or dismissive? I took such complaints to the staff team, or, if they were more sensitive in nature, just to the churchwardens. They could then help me sift the concerns to see which were valid and needed addressing by me or others, and which were not. This was very important support, and helped me remain sensitive to the needs of the church without becoming discouraged by criticism.

Cultivate Leaders: The Ingredients

So how are we to identify and develop leaders? It is a topic about which the Bible has much to say. It tells us about the lives of leaders such as Abraham, Joseph and Moses; Joshua, Deborah and Samuel; Saul, David and Solomon; Jesus, Peter and Paul – and on the list could go. But if we want criteria by which to identify leaders, the book of Acts and the Pastoral Epistles (1 and 2 Timothy and Titus) may be the most immediately helpful. These are directed at those we often call "ordained ministers," and most Christian leaders are not called to that. However, they do highlight the qualities God seeks in leadership, which makes them a good place to start.

Three major titles emerge in the New Testament for those who were to lead the church after the apostolic era: deacons, presbyters or elders, and overseers. In some denominations, including the Roman Catholic Church, Orthodox Churches and the Anglican Communion, the word "presbyter" is contracted to "priest," and the role of the "overseer" is termed "bishop." Other churches and denominations use terms such as "minister" or "pastor." How these different titles and roles have developed over the history of the church is not our concern here. Instead, the question is: How were these leaders identified?

Identifying Leadership Qualities

Deacons

Acts 6 tells us that the work of deacons was originally to serve at tables for widows so that the apostles could concentrate on prayer and the ministry of the Word (Acts 6:3–4). Deacons had an important ministry, and those called needed to be "of good standing, full of the Spirit and of wisdom" (v. 3). We read that "they chose Stephen, a man full of faith and the Holy Spirit, together with Philip, Prochorus, Nicanor, Timon, Parmenas, and Nicolaus, a proselyte of Antioch. They had these men stand before the apostles, who prayed and laid their hands on them" (vv. 5–6).

We get a fuller list of qualifications for the role of deacon in 1 Timothy:

> Deacons likewise must be serious, not double-tongued, not indulging in much wine, not greedy for money; they must hold fast to the mystery of the faith with a clear conscience. And let them first be tested; then, if they prove themselves blameless, let them serve as deacons. Women likewise must be serious, not slanderers, but temperate, faithful in all things. Let deacons be married only once, and let them manage their children and their households well; for those who serve well as deacons gain a good standing for themselves and great boldness in the faith that is in Christ Jesus. (3:8–13)

It is striking how many of these requirements are about character and home life: dignity, honesty, self-control in the use of alcohol, avoidance of dishonest gain, faithfulness in marriage ("married only once" in v. 12 may be best understood as "husband of one wife") and raising their children well. As leadership coach James Lawrence points out, leadership is learned in the home.[3] This resonates with Paul's instruction to Timothy, "Do not speak harshly to an older man, but speak to him as to a father, to younger men as brothers, to older women as mothers, to younger women as sisters – with absolute purity" (1 Tim 5:1–2). There is a call for a firm faith, but the emphasis is on a life that reveals that faith in action. They need to be tested first, suggesting they are required to have had experience of other ministries beforehand, and to have been recognized as people of genuine faith, whose whole lives testify to what they believe.

---

3. James Lawrence, *Growing Leaders: Reflections on Leadership, Life and Jesus* (Abingdon: Bible Reading Fellowship, 2004), 171.

This is important for our discernment of leaders. They must be men and women of faith in Christ, but they should also be people whose faith is demonstrated in their lives. Is there evidence of the fruit of the Spirit, enabling them to be self-controlled in their speech, their use of alcohol and their handling of money? We need to see this before they are given leadership roles in our churches. Issues of worldly prestige, personal appearance or local popularity should not be allowed to trump these concerns if we are to follow this biblical teaching. Nor should we bring someone into leadership in an attempt to address his or her pastoral needs. Leaders need to be chosen for their potential to lead.

Elders and Overseers

Then there are the elders and overseers whose roles did not seem to be sharply distinguished in New Testament times. They were given major leadership responsibilities in the early church. When Paul addressed the Ephesian elders he told them to

> Keep watch over yourselves and over all the flock, of which the Holy Spirit has made you overseers, to shepherd the church of God that he obtained with the blood of his own Son. I know that after I have gone, savage wolves will come in among you, not sparing the flock. Some even from your own group will come distorting the truth in order to entice the disciples to follow them. Therefore be alert, remembering that for three years I did not cease night or day to warn everyone with tears. (Acts 20:28–31)

The work of these elders, also called "overseers" in verse 28, was to be shepherds of God's flock, an idea which is repeated in 1 Peter 5:2. The metaphor of the shepherd is one that Jesus famously took to himself (John 10:11), fulfilling Old Testament hopes for a leader who would provide daily sustenance for God's people, protect them from harm, and take them where they should go (see Ps 23). What a wonderful description of a Christian leader, who is called to be an under-shepherd of Jesus Christ himself.

A more detailed list of qualifications for elders and overseers is given by Paul to Titus, when he explains:

> I left you behind in Crete for this reason, that you should put in order what remained to be done, and should appoint elders in every town, as I directed you: someone who is blameless, married only once, whose children are believers, not accused of debauchery and not rebellious. For a bishop, as God's steward,

> must be blameless; he must not be arrogant or quick-tempered or addicted to wine or violent or greedy for gain; but he must be hospitable, a lover of goodness, prudent, upright, devout, and self-controlled. He must have a firm grasp of the word that is trustworthy in accordance with the teaching, so that he may be able both to preach with sound doctrine and to refute those who contradict it. (Titus 1:5–9)

Some of these points are echoed in what Paul wrote to Timothy in Ephesus:

> The saying is sure: whoever aspires to the office of bishop desires a noble task. Now a bishop must be above reproach, married only once, temperate, sensible, respectable, hospitable, an apt teacher, not a drunkard, not violent but gentle, not quarrelsome, and not a lover of money. He must manage his own household well, keeping his children submissive and respectful in every way – for if someone does not know how to manage his own household, how can he take care of God's church? He must not be a recent convert, or he may be puffed up with conceit and fall into the condemnation of the devil. Moreover, he must be well thought of by outsiders, so that he may not fall into disgrace and the snare of the devil. (1 Tim 3:1–7)

Once again, it is the character qualities that stand out: above reproach, the husband of one wife, not arrogant, or short-tempered, or a drunkard, or violent, or greedy, but self-controlled, upright and holy. There are some skills required too, such as being hospitable, able to teach the faith, and able to rebuke those who contradict it. But these cannot stand alone without the Christian character that supports them. There is to be no public/private divide here, as some would recommend. The prohibition against recent converts, and the need for a good reputation with outsiders, highlight the importance of allowing time for the genuineness of their Christian commitment to be seen. Sometimes a person may appear very suitable for leadership, and only later does it become clear that there are some character issues that would need to be addressed before that person should be given the responsibilities of leadership. Such things as hospitality invite people into our inner world, our family and our friends, and that is where integrity, or the lack of it, is often revealed. Drunkenness, and the violence associated with it, has no place in the Christian home or in Christian leadership. Gentleness and peace should be hallmarks instead. Nor is there any place for greed, which was evident among the false teachers Timothy was dealing with in Ephesus (1 Tim 6:5). These things bring the church into disrepute, so we should allow time for discernment first. This is why Paul says, "Do not ordain anyone hastily" (1 Tim 5:22).

The issue of the behaviour of the children of believers is a sensitive one. Many Christian leaders, including some who have proved highly effective over many years, have one or more children who are not believers. Does Titus 1:6, "whose children are believers," disqualify them? This is a delicate subject, and many have wrestled with it.[4] On the one hand, it is clear that those who would be leaders in God's church and have children at home need to take seriously their calling to raise them in the faith. They should give time to reading the Bible and praying with them, trying to live out lives of godliness, sharing stories of what God is doing, and not burdening them inappropriately with their frustrations and difficulties.

On the other hand, we cannot make our children become Christians, or stay faithful to Christ if they do. They may come to faith only later in life, or have a period of time as a prodigal son or daughter. A judgement call is needed here. If someone's children are unbelievers, is that a sign of negligence on the part of the parent? Does it reveal a lack of integrity? If so, it is best picked up now, before those failings affect the wider congregation once that person is in leadership. However, if that does not seem to be the case, this verse should not be regarded as a basis for disqualifying people from leadership. Such poignant, persistent parental frustrations may be used by God to deepen their commitment to prayer, humble them under the Lord's sovereign care, keep them mindful of those who are currently lost, and stir up a passion for evangelism.

Cultivating the Character of a Leader

Identifying leaders is therefore primarily about noticing Christian character. That means that the development of leaders is going to be largely about Christian character formation. So the task of the leader in search of other leaders is part of his or her wider role as disciple-maker. Yes, there are specific abilities that need to be discerned and exercised, such as shepherding, teaching, rebuking and offering hospitality, but those will not be sufficient on their own. The emphasis is on Christian character and the evidence of the fruit of the Spirit in their lives.

---

4. See Robert S. Rayburn and Steven A. Nicoletti, "An Elder Must Have Believing Children: Titus 1:6 and a Neglected Case of Conscience," *Presbyterion* 43, no. 2 (Fall 2017): 69–80; and John Stott, *The Message of 1 Timothy and Titus* (Leicester: Inter-Varsity Press, 1998), 176.

Realizing that everything we do in the regular cycle of church life to promote godliness of character can help raise up leaders for Christ's church should be an encouragement for all those engaged in preaching, teaching and pastoral care. As we get alongside those who are growing in their faith, we can be prayerfully discerning whether there are places where they can start to move into leadership. Such responsibilities may well help accelerate their growth as disciples.

In his research on leadership, John P. Kotter noticed the importance of allowing leaders to face challenges early on.[5] I am so glad, looking back, that I was allowed to lead, or co-lead, Christian groups from the age of thirteen. I still remember the way those experiences engaged me in my Christian walk, and helped me to see the power of prayer. They also taught me a lot about leadership. So much growth in leadership is through experience, and by mentors who can help us reflect on that experience. It has been observed that people learn 70 percent from job-related experiences, 20 percent through interactions with others, and 10 percent from formal educational events.[6] Experience really is our greatest teacher. If you think someone may have leadership gifts, why not let that person have some small leadership role, support him or her in that work, and see how he or she does?

The character formation we are describing here sometimes comes about very painfully, through suffering that produces hope: "We also boast in our sufferings, knowing that suffering produces endurance, and endurance produces character, and character produces hope, and hope does not disappoint us, because God's love has been poured into our hearts through the Holy Spirit that has been given to us" (Rom 5:3–5). Lessons learned through suffering go deep and can transform our character. They can instil a humble, godly hopefulness about the future, despite all the challenges of life, and that is a great help to any leader.

Leadership experts Warren Bennis and Robert Thomas speak about the "crucibles of leadership" that are so often part of what enables someone to grow into an outstanding leader.[7] Joseph and Moses, two of the most striking

5. John P. Kotter, "What Leaders Really Do," in Harvard Business Review, *HBR's 10 Must Reads on Leadership* (Boston: Harvard Business Review Press, 2011), 37.

6. Michael M. Lombardo and Robert W. Eichinger, *The Career Architect Development Planner*, 1st ed. (Minneapolis: Lominger, 1996), iv.

7. Warren G. Bennis and Robert J. Thomas, "The Crucibles of Leadership," in Harvard Business Review, *HBR's 10 Must Reads on Leadership*, 97–113.

leaders in the Old Testament, spent years in obscurity, whether in prison or serving as a shepherd (Gen 39–41; Exod 3). They must have wondered what their lives had come to in those wilderness years. But there is little doubt that they learned a great deal from those difficult times. If we can harness the lessons learned from our own crucibles of leadership, and help others to harness theirs, it will be hugely beneficial.

Spotting Potential Leaders

But how are we to spot those people who might have the potential for leadership? Many Christian leaders have written on this topic, but we might summarise their findings in the following questions:

1. Do they have *integrity*, with a character that is humble, prayerful, honest, teachable and stable, as they walk with God in the light of his Word and the power of his Spirit?
2. Do they take *initiatives*?
3. Do they *influence* others?
4. Do they have the *intuition* necessary for good people skills?
5. Do they have the *intelligence* required to make sense of situations and to know what to do next?

We have already considered the importance of "integrity" and what it involves in terms of being trustworthy. When it comes to spotting "initiative," it is a matter of seeing if they notice when something needs to be done, and do something about it without being asked. It could be as simple as moving chairs or opening a door. "Influence" is then seen in whether others follow their lead, perhaps by helping move chairs or holding the door open. "Intuition" is harder to spot, but might best be seen in how well they engage in conversation with people of all ages and abilities. The "intelligence" we seek might not be revealed in qualifications or prior experience, since it is more a matter of wisdom than knowledge. This could be assessed by talking with them about leadership issues, without betraying confidences, and seeing what response they would suggest. These are all things that can be assessed without putting people into leadership positions, so they can be observed prior to being entrusted with those responsibilities.

Ken Kamau, Senior Pastor of Kileleshwa Covenant Community Church, Nairobi, Kenya, comes to a strikingly similar set of conclusions about what we are looking for in leaders with his five Cs: Character, Chemistry, Competence, Capacity and Calling.[8] "Character" is his name for what we have called "integrity." "Chemistry" is about how well someone would fit in with the leadership team, so it is somewhat similar to "intuition." "Competence" is about the ability to get things done, so that parallels "intelligence." "Capacity" is "the emotional, psychological and spiritual capacity to step into a new venture and give their best regardless of circumstances,"[9] which is a measure of maturity, and might be similar to taking "initiative" and "influence" together. "Calling" is somewhat taken for granted in our list above but deserves to be emphasized, since someone with all of these other qualities who lacks a sense of call to leadership is not in a position to lead at this point. It is vital that leaders want to lead, or are at least are willing to do so, if they believe they are called to lead.

One of my greatest joys in Christian ministry is seeing people develop in their leadership roles. I have watched people grow in the leadership of children's ministries, youth work, churches, schools, businesses and other organizations. Working in theological education in the USA and UK has allowed me the delight of watching leaders mature to the point where they can serve at a high level. Someone has estimated that in thirty years of ministry a pastor can touch 100,000 lives! That is a lot of influence. And all leaders have influence, be it greater or less than that. What a privilege it is to cultivate leaders!

In some African and Asian contexts, leaders may be in place because they are community leaders, such as a village head, not because of their Christian faith. This presents its own challenges. While their insights will be valuable because of their knowledge of the community, there is a danger that distinctly Christian visions and values may not readily resonate with them. If possible, take time with them individually to build up trust and to share more personally what you are hoping to see happen, and how that will benefit the community. Do be praying for them, their family and their friends, and bear witness to your faith as and when appropriate.

Developing the Skills of a Leader

Once we have spotted potential leaders with the required character qualities, we can look for those skills of shepherding, teaching, rebuking and offering hospitality, and see what further development might be necessary. Not every

8. Ken Kamau, *First Things First: Growing in Pastoral Ministry* (Nairobi: HippoBooks, 2016), 74–75.

9. Kamau, *First Things First*, 75.

leader will feel he or she has the gift of *hospitality*, but those who aspire to leadership will need to learn to be hospitable since so much of their work of meeting people and disciple-making will rely on it. They might benefit from guidance on how to make their offices and homes into welcoming places, and by being delivered from worry about visitors coming to judge them. Offering drinks and snacks to help guests feel comfortable and free to talk can easily be learned even by those who don't have a gift of hospitality. Where they don't feel comfortable cooking, these leaders-in-training can be encouraged to ask someone else to cook, or to order food in when necessary. These practical skills can be developed with practice. After all, it is not about offering elaborate meals, but about creating a space which is conducive to talk and prayer.

The abilities to shepherd a group, to teach and where necessary to rebuke are probably best learned from shadowing more experienced leaders. To learn the skill of *shepherding*, aspiring leaders could become members of a small group led by others, then be made assistant leaders, and finally be given responsibility for a group with ongoing mentoring. I had the opportunity to do that in school and university Christian Unions. Others may have such opportunities at Christian camps, Bible classes and in churches. These are highly significant incubators of leaders. A great many of today's Christian leaders owe a debt of gratitude to such forms of preparation to be shepherds.

Likewise, potential leaders should learn to *teach*, either because their future work will involve teaching or because, as leaders, they will need to explain what they are thinking with regard to their vision and the steps needed to bring it about. They can learn this skill from watching others teach children, young people or adults, and then having the chance to teach them themselves. I spent two years as a physics teacher after graduating from university. It was a baptism of fire in many ways, especially since I was a rather young-looking twenty-one-year-old and was often teaching eighteen-year-olds who looked older than me. But I learned a huge amount about having a clear educational goal and planning how to deliver it in ways that provoked interest and engagement, with carefully prepared notes that I could develop from year to year. If there were subjects that were not clear to me, I simply had to work on them until I understood them, or I would not be able to communicate them to the teenagers. Especially when teaching new material, it is often the teacher who learns the most. What an opportunity this is for a novice leader, not only to learn the craft of teaching, but to discover more about the faith and how to share it at the same time.

Rebuking can be one of the hardest skills to learn, though it is essential for leaders. This is probably best learned from leaders who are more experienced at it, or from professional training in how to have such a concerned conversation. I learned a lot about it from my two years of teaching, although those approaches had to be substantially rethought for correcting adults. We will return to this topic in Phase 4 when we consider how to coach leaders in these skills. All these experiences should help leaders grow in knowledge, confidence and self-awareness, which will be very helpful to them as they develop. Such self-awareness is identified by Daniel Goleman as one of the five key elements of emotional intelligence needed by leaders,[10] along with self-regulation, motivation, empathy and social skills.

Coordinating the Roles of the Leaders

If there are a number of teams being led by different leaders, there needs to be some way of coordinating them for maximum effectiveness. There should be an overall leadership team, under the governing council, to oversee the day-to-day work of the church or organization, like the Ministry Leadership Team at St Helen's. Having other leaders report directly or indirectly to someone on that team can be helpful. That way, those involved with any aspect of the organization feel they have a voice at the decision-making table, and there are ready-made channels of communication to allow information to flow freely to it and from it. Laying out the structure in an organization chart can be a helpful way to display who reports to whom, and not only helps orientate anyone who is new to the organization, but also assists those already in it to make good use of the structure.

Conclusion

Cultivating and nurturing leadership is time consuming, but it is vital and exciting work. It is really about making disciples who make disciples, and being made more of a disciple in the process. It is a ministry of multiplication, not only for the church or organization you lead, but for other churches and organizations too. We shall see later how to make good use of these leaders. Here we are concerned with the need for mounting the search and making it an everyday part of your life as a leader to be on the lookout for other leaders and to do all in your power to help them grow in that God-given gifting.

Raising up leaders like this leaves a lasting legacy. Egyptian Christian businessman Khaled Bichara died on Friday, 31 January 2020 at the age of

10. Daniel Goleman, "What Makes a Leader?," *Harvard Business Review* (January 2004): 82–91, https://thisisthrive.com/sites/default/files/What-Makes-a-Leader-Daniel-Goleman.pdf.

forty-eight. He was described as the Bill Gates of Egypt after a remarkable business career in the communications field, which included being Group Chief Executive Officer of Orascom Telecom Holding. What was less well known was the amount of time he spent mentoring other leaders, especially entrepreneurs wanting to start businesses in Egypt. The extent of this investment became clear only after news spread of his fatal car accident and posts flooded social media from those who had benefited from his care. Many could not have done what they did without him. Leaders know what it takes to lead, and have great opportunities to invest in other leaders. It does take time, but it is time well spent.

Taking It Further

How might you grow as a leader in cultivating other leaders?

1. Who do you know who is already in leadership? Pick three to five people.
   (a) What qualities serve them well in those roles?
   (b) Can you think of other areas where their leadership would thrive?
   (c) What might be a good next opportunity for each of them?
   (d) How might you help prepare them for these roles?

2. Who do you know who is not currently in leadership but might have the right aptitudes? Pick another three to five people, if possible.
   (a) What would you suggest for their first steps into leadership?
   (b) Where might their leadership best be deployed in the future?
   (c) What knowledge, skills or character issues would each of them need to work on for those possibilities to be realized?
   (d) How might you help them develop as leaders to the fullest extent?

Phase 3

Discern Vision

Once trust has been established and leaders identified, you can move to the third phase of leadership: discerning vision. By this point you have become established as a leader, you have got to know the history and present situation of the church or organization, and you have a team of leaders, some of whom have been identified as the senior leadership team. Let us also assume that by this point there is a measure of peace that allows sufficient calmness for vision formation. If people are still very anxious about some of the pressing issues of the church or organization, it is hard to spend time thinking about the long-term future. For lower levels of unease, however, such a vision-discernment process may be just the thing to bring about greater peace and fruitfulness.

Once you are at this stage, it is time to clarify what the future would be like if the church or organization were really to thrive. How would you describe it in five- or ten-years' time if it fulfilled its God-given potential? That is the vision question. Once you can answer it, you can unite people around that common goal and make sure everything the church or organization does moves it in that direction. It assists you in your mission and ministry, in staff recruitment and development, and in fundraising and stewarding your resources. It becomes a great blessing to the leader and to the whole organization.

The vision on its own, however, is not enough. It provides the answer to the question "Where do we believe God is leading us?" but it does not explain why you should go, or how you should get there. So a leader needs not only to articulate a vision, but ideally also to state the purpose, which answers the "why" question, and the core values, which answer the "how" question. Then you have:

- *Vision:* where you are going, and what you are to become if you follow the path God is leading you on;
- *Purpose:* why your church or organization exists; and
- *Core values:* how you should carry out that purpose.

For Moses, the vision was to see the people of God living in the promised land. That was *where* they were going. Their purpose in making that journey was to depend on God's daily guidance and provision through the wilderness to bear witness to the glory and faithfulness of God among the nations. That was *why* they were going. The core values that guided them on their way were to be love, in response to God's love in delivering them from slavery in Egypt; trust, in the God who had proved to be so trustworthy; and obedience, which put that love and trust into action (see Deut 30:16). This was *how* they were to make the journey: lovingly, trustingly and obediently. Vision, purpose and core values are invaluable to a leader, and discerning them is one of the most important things a leader does. These three things together enable the leader to chart the course for the journey that lies ahead.

I still remember when I first heard about vision, purpose and core values in the business world, and I must admit that I was highly sceptical about them. They seemed somewhat artificial and superfluous. It was only as I saw them put to use that I recognized their potential. I also had reservations about them being used in a Christian context, fearing they might make it too much like a business and diminish the sense of daily dependency on divine direction. It is only as I have come to use them in a church and in theological education that I have seen how helpful they can be in discerning that divine direction and in sharing it with others.

There are, of course, many thriving churches and organizations that have not stated their vision, purpose or core values, so they are clearly not indispensable. However, in my experience of such organizations, they generally do have these things, but they are implicit rather than explicit. A perceptive newcomer would eventually be able to suggest what they were. For such churches and organizations, I would suggest the benefit of stating vision, purpose and core values lies primarily in communicating them more clearly, both internally and externally, and I have come to believe that would be a good investment of time.

Discern Vision: A Case Study

Vision

The moment I first realized that we needed to discern vision at St Helen's Church came when we were in a position to add one or two members of staff and were wondering how to go about it. What would we need to do to ensure their work was coordinated with what was already going on? We brought in a work consultant from the Church Pastoral Aid Society, Laurence Gamlen, who was very helpful in addressing this problem. The first question he asked was, "What is your vision?" We rummaged around in the records and found a vision statement from years gone by, but had to admit that we really weren't being influenced by it any more. It had been too ambitious. So the consultant helped us refine that longer vision statement into one that really caught hold and was hugely helpful to us. Looking back, we should really have had that vision in place before deciding who we needed to recruit, to be sure we were developing a staff team to deliver on our purpose, not just how best to integrate them. But even at this stage it was a great help.

We started this vision-discernment process by asking two questions:

- What has happened in the history of this church that might indicate where God is taking us, as we prayerfully discern God's vision for our future?
- What would it look like if the things we long to see happen in this church came to pass? How would it then be described?

These questions helped us to state what it would be like if the church found its maturity. It was a vision of a preferred future. The process began with a lot of prayer and consultation among a small group of leaders, who formulated a draft vision statement. We then shared that statement with other leaders and members of the congregation, and refined it repeatedly until there was a sense of ownership.

The statement we ended up with was: "Our vision is to be a caring church that reaches out, demonstrating that Jesus lives and changes lives." That was short enough to be remembered, but significant enough to be inspiring. We wanted to see that happen.

Once the vision statement was approved, it was a matter of communicating it to the congregations. We had a sermon series based on it, and teaching on it for all ages. We used it on our letterhead, put it on our noticeboards, and mentioned it whenever the opportunity arose. We made cards to place in a wallet or handbag so church members could remember it and use it to invite others to services. The vision expressed what we were aiming at as a church community, and we used that statement often.

The vision statement really helped to unify and galvanize the church. It allowed us to see what St Helen's Church would look like if all our different energies were brought together and we got to the place where we thought God was taking us. It also had a rallying effect externally, as we were able to say to people, "Here is our vision. Is that exciting to you? Do you want to be part of it?" It helped recruit and orientate staff by clarifying what we were trying to do. And it helped set priorities for how we spent our time and money. If something did not move us towards the vision, we might not need to do it. In fact, it was probably better if we didn't.

Purpose

Then there was the task of asking: What is the underlying purpose of the church if that is its vision? Here again our consultant was helpful, enabling us to take the purpose of every church – to make disciples of all nations (Matt 28:19) – and explain what that meant specifically for this church. No doubt we were to be engaged in worship, learning, fellowship, evangelism and acts of service, but what in particular were we to be doing? Why were we there at all? We ended up with not one but three purpose statements:

1. To grow in our experience of God as committed disciples
2. To grow in love and care for each other as a Christian body
3. To serve the community and share the good news of Jesus in the world

The first was mainly directed vertically towards God and in response to God. The second was orientated more inwardly regarding the life of the congregation and how we learned to care for one another so we could care for the wider world. And the third was more outward-looking, about how to reach the community around us and bring the gospel of Jesus Christ to them. It can be summarized as looking up, looking in, and looking out. We used these purpose statements frequently. In his best-selling *Purpose Driven Church*, Rick Warren, Senior Pastor of Saddleback Church, California, USA, recommends finding ways to repeat the purpose of the church at least monthly.[1] Then it can gradually become embedded in the life of the congregations.

Core Values

By this point, St Helen's had a sense of *where* we thought God was taking us (our vision), and *why* we thought this should come about (our purpose), but

1. Rick Warren, *The Purpose Driven Church: Growth without Compromising Your Message and Mission* (Grand Rapids, MI: Zondervan, 1995), 111–119.

that left the question *how*? How would we go about it? What would guide us day by day as we carried out our purpose to achieve our vision? For this we needed to articulate the values we prized above all others. We never really stated those core values at St Helen's. I only came to learn the importance of stating them while leading Trinity School for Ministry. But if I were to suggest what the core values of St Helen's Church were, I would say:

1. Raising young people in the Christian faith
2. Growing disciples of Jesus Christ
3. Supplying leadership for the wider church
4. Supporting world mission

There was clearly a strong emphasis on children's and youth ministry, with many groups meeting throughout the week to serve that age group. A lot of energy was going into those ministries. It was also very clear that there was a concern about discipleship and a commitment to lifelong learning. In addition, there was a remarkable history of St Helen's raising up ordained leaders out of a relatively small congregation. And there was a surprisingly large number of missionaries who had gone to serve overseas. Those were at least four of the core values the congregation held dear, and that guided how we lived out our purpose. Such values clarify what makes a church what it is, and help people see how they can contribute to its growth and development.

When I became principal of Trinity School for Ministry, the purpose statement was already in place. We were "forming Christian leaders for mission." That was a great statement, which provided clarity about our task with wonderful brevity. The core values were worked out on a retreat day as part of the recruitment process which brought me into the leadership position, since the search committee was aware that they needed to state the values clearly to see if they were shared by applicants. The council members, faculty and major stakeholders came together for a day to pray, brainstorm and craft statements that described Trinity's values. Each one was carefully explained, but the headings for the core values that emerged were:

1. Evangelical and Anglican identity
2. Welcoming evangelical, charismatic and catholic streams of the church
3. Serving the church
4. Excellent teaching and scholarship

5. Deep formation in community
6. Being a school of discipleship
7. Lifelong learning
8. Trusting God's provision

These core value statements helped us establish the organizational culture at Trinity, spelling out what it stood for and what we treasured most. They articulated what might be encouraged and what might not be, where effort would be expended and where it wouldn't. They also had a special value when significant changes were anticipated. They proved especially helpful in considering possible partnerships with Lutheran and Presbyterian denominations, with other colleges, with churches, and with a student ministry. It was crucial that we shared those core values if the partnership was to work. Those values also proved fruitful in helping those partnerships prosper.

The vision statement for Trinity School for Ministry came about later, with considerable help from one of our council members who had done this work previously for a multinational electric company. At the start of my second year as principal, a team of council members, faculty and alumni began to meet weekly to chart how the college had been used by God down the years, using the six previous principals to describe the eras of its life. After that we asked ourselves, "If that trajectory is maintained, where does it seem the Lord is leading us?" And, "If we were to describe the end result of this journey in the way we hope it will turn out, what would we say?"

One of our struggles was how to include our commitment to evangelical Anglicanism without suggesting that our vision was to see everyone become an evangelical Anglican. That would have contradicted our second value, to welcome different streams of the church, and it would have restricted our vision. It would also have lost a sense of the ecumenism that is inherent to both evangelicalism and Anglicanism. A breakthrough in this process occurred when we realized that we could simply describe our task as being an evangelical seminary in the Anglican tradition before we got to state the main part of the vision. We ended up with a vision statement that was really both an identity statement in its first sentence, explaining who we were, and a vision statement in the second, stating where we were going:

> Trinity School for Ministry is an evangelical seminary in the Anglican tradition. In this fractured world, we desire to be a global centre for Christian formation, producing outstanding leaders who can plant, renew, and grow churches that make disciples of Jesus Christ.

If we had to go to the heart of it, the vision statement was simply: "to be a global centre for Christian formation." But that whole vision statement, starting with its identity statement, proved to be hugely valuable, and it is a format I would recommend to others.

It was amazing to me how well that vision statement worked for us. It helped us fix our eyes on an exciting future. Along with the purpose statement and core values, it played a major role in guiding the college's leadership and governing council in their deliberations, in the recruitment and motivation of faculty and staff, and in fundraising and the stewardship of resources. All the work that went into producing those statements was amply rewarded. I suspect it usually is.

When I had the privilege of teaching at the Anglican Leadership Institute in South Carolina, USA, in January 2018, delegates were invited to share the vision, purpose and core values from the ministries they represented. Each of them is very different and sheds light on the benefit of stating your vision, purpose and core values. Here is what some of them said:

- Mike Adegbile, Executive Director of Nigeria Evangelical Missions Association, gave their vision as "to see God glorified as all the expressions of the global church are mobilized as a global mission force and synergized to finish the task of world evangelization." For their purpose, he stated, "We exist as a network to facilitate community among mobilizers through communications, cooperation and collaboration." The association's core values are "collaboration and synergy, unity in diversity, partnerships, catalysing mobilization, best practices, the centrality of the local church, supporting organizations, and global mission."
- Francis Barongo, Archdeacon of Kitari Diocese, Uganda, had a personal vision: "to have a Christ-centred ministry that is to alleviate human suffering and give glory to God." His purpose was to "maintain hard work to harness resources around you," and core values of "faithfulness, hard work, self-discipline, welcome to visitors, and raising a stable family that glorifies God."
- Eraste Bigirimana, Bishop of Bujumbura, Burundi, shared their diocesan vision: "the community transformed by the gospel and committed to their holistic development." Their purpose is to carry out the five marks of mission of the Anglican Communion: "To proclaim the good news of the kingdom; to teach, baptize and nurture new believers; to respond to human need by loving service; to seek to transform unjust structures of society, to challenge

violence of every kind and to pursue peace and reconciliation; and to strive to safeguard the integrity of creation and sustain and renew the life of the earth." The diocese's core values are "love, compassion and solidarity."

- Henok Hariyanto, Cluster-Head of the Anglican Church in the Riau Archipelago in Indonesia, said his vision was to "establish a parish," and his purpose, "to be committed in worship, evangelism, discipleship, fellowship and mission."
- James Kennedy, Team Rector of Chipping Norton in the Cotswolds, England, with oversight of nine churches, said their vision is "love – broaden and deepen our gathered worship and prayer; serve – extend our outreach, especially to vulnerable families; and grow – invest in personal discipleship through small groups." Their purpose is "to share the life-changing love of Jesus, serving our whole community." The core values which guide them are "relationship, worship and welcome (what we believe); family, nurture and growth (who we are and where we are aiming); and community, witness and service (what we are doing)."
- Godwin Makabi, Rector of the Christian Institute, a theological college of the Anglican Diocese of Jos, Nigeria, said their vision is "to be a seminary where students are equipped (to know God and love him) for the work of ministry and for building up the body of Christ spiritually, numerically, physically, intellectually and economically." Their purpose is "to raise young people who will get involved in the Great Commission: mission, evangelism and outreach. This includes local mission in their immediate area of residence, in other parts of Nigeria, in Africa, and in other parts of the world as the Lord may call upon them to do." The college's core values were "being excellent in the holistic development of students, with emphasis on discipline, integrity and service, and with prayer and worship at the centre of their lives."
- Francis Matumba, Diocesan Training Chaplain in the Diocese of Lake Malawi, Malawi, shared the diocesan vision: "to be a caring and prayerful church that lives according to the Word of God for the salvation of mankind." Their purpose is "to bring salvation and spiritual growth to the diocesan community and beyond, through evangelism, discipleship and social-economic development." The diocese's core values are "Scripture, integrity and honesty,

stewardship and giving, sacraments and liturgical traditions, and the practice of humility."

- There was also a vision statement for Katundu Nursery School, Katundu, which was "Reduction of illiteracy in remote areas," with the purpose of "enabling young girls to know how to read the Word of God." The underlying concern is that only 45 percent of young people can read and write.
- Sam Parddy, Archdeacon in the Diocese of Kofoidua in Ghana, said their vision was "to put up a church building"; their purpose, "to raise leaders and workers to build the church"; and their core values were "prayer, trust, patience, steadfastness, boldness, love, kindness and unity."
- Greg Snyder, Rector of St John's Church, St John's Island, South Carolina, USA, shared their vision of being "a parish family that cares for the community, prepares disciples for global ministry, shares the healing grace of Jesus Christ, and declares the power of the Holy Spirit," which he pointed out fitted well with the diocese's vision of "making biblical Anglicans for a global age."

These vision and purpose statements and lists of core values are not always being used in the same way. They sometimes have a wide target, such as a nation or the world, and at other times a narrower focus of a diocese, a church or a task, such as erecting a church building. However, whichever way they are used, the most important thing is that they bring clarity and cohesion to the work that is to be done, and help leaders fulfil their divine calling in that place.

Discern Vision: The Ingredients

As we have seen, when trust has been established and senior leaders identified, it is a good moment to discern vision and work out what purpose and core values that entails. Perhaps you are on a team of church planters and it is time to describe what kind of church you think the Lord is calling you to plant. It may be that you are on the leadership team of an established church or organization and you are seeking greater clarity on what the future might look like. Or your leadership may be in a school, college or university, or you may oversee a local, national or international ministry and want to articulate a vision for where you think God wants you to be in five- or ten-years' time. How do you go about doing that?

It would probably be wise to engage a consultant for this work if that is possible, as we did at St Helen's. Finding the right consultant can itself be a challenge, so it is worth looking at the options and getting references from those who have engaged them before to assess their suitability. Whether you engage a consultant or not, however, it might be helpful to know what this process normally entails and to imagine your own role in it. We shall start with vision and then move to purpose and core values.

Discerning a Vision

The first step is to be sure you *have the agreement of the governing council* that this is the right moment to work on the vision, purpose and core values, and that you have their support for the proposed process for doing so, which might be like the one laid out below.[2] The council is well placed to see if this is the right time for such an undertaking, and should play a guiding role in the process. This can be a lot of work, and it might be wise to think in terms of addressing only the vision, the purpose or the core values to begin with, starting with whichever would be most helpful.

We should be aware that this call for group discernment may run counter to the views of leadership held by some. They remember events such as Abraham receiving a vision from God about becoming a great nation (Gen 12), and Moses receiving a vision from God for rescuing his people from slavery and taking them to the promised land (Exod 3). Such things clearly do happen still, and they need to be received with thanksgiving. But I do not think this is the way God always works. Sometimes God gives us the overall vision, like that of the new heaven and earth of Revelation 21 and 22, and a global mission, the Great Commission, of Matthew 28:16–20, and calls us to discern what part we are to play in them. Perhaps that is how the apostle Paul planned his missionary journeys to the Gentiles. The Lord also supplies us with counsellors, often other leaders, so that we can seek God's wisdom together. As it says in the book of Proverbs, "Without counsel, plans go wrong, but with many advisers they succeed" (Prov 15:22).

The second step is to *assemble your key leaders*. Probably six to eight people is the ideal number. They need to be people of prayer who will see it as their

2. For a more detailed process, I recommend James Lawrence, *Growing Leaders: Reflections on Leadership, Life and Jesus* (Abingdon: Bible Reading Fellowship, 2004), 197–213. Alternatively, you might like to try the "Appreciative Inquiry" approach, focused on what has been, and continues to be, most appreciated about your organization, to help chart the future. See https://www.centerforappreciativeinquiry.net for more information.

primary task to seek the Lord's will for the future. This team should be well aware of the major ministries of the church or organization, and include a good mixture of gender, race and age so that, if possible, any member of the church, ministry or organization can look at this team and see that it is aware of the things that matter to him or her. It is a great help if one or more of the team have done such vision-formation work before, whether in a Christian setting or elsewhere. Someone with business experience of this kind might be delighted to see his or her skills put to such use.[3] At St Helen's, we were revising rather than creating a vision statement, which was less demanding. I worked with the churchwardens, the worship leader, the children's ministry leader, the parish evangelist and the pastoral care coordinator to produce an initial draft, under the guidance of our consultant. Choosing the team carefully was important, although it is helpful to remember that others will be drawn into the process along the way.

The third step is to *research the past in order to detect a trajectory into the future.* Here a helpful question is: "What has God blessed in this church or organization in the past?" This is often a clue for what lies ahead. It may help to ask this question of previous eras, perhaps broken down by decade or by the years of different overall leaders. Have there been previous vision statements that you could build on? Are there major themes that emerge repeatedly, such as evangelism, care for the homeless or international mission? Those are also worth keeping for when you develop the statement of core values. The next question is: "Where might the Lord be leading us?" This points towards a vision statement.

The fourth step is to begin putting together the ingredients you have collected and *try to boil the ideas down to a single sentence.* This is probably the hardest part. It is when the main findings from the previous step are distilled into a draft vision statement. At this stage, it is very important to bring in every possible constituency of the church or organization, especially their leaders, as well as the governing council, to give feedback on this draft statement. There may be many iterations of this process as new drafts of a vision statement are suggested and shared. Sometimes this work can be done in a matter of days, as I saw happen when the Overseas Council of Australia worked with the governing council of the Alexandria School of Theology in Cairo to discern their vision. Often, however, the process takes weeks or even

3. See Richard J. Goossen and R. Paul Stevens, *Entrepreneurial Leadership: Finding Your Calling, Making a Difference* (Downers Grove, IL: InterVarsity Press, 2013), 164–170, on involving entrepreneurs in the life of the church.

months. Eventually, some resolution is needed. Unanimity may not be possible. In the end the leaders, especially the senior leaders, need to own the vision and use it, so they need to take a lead. If the process is a success, the statement should allow you to articulate a compelling vision that energizes people. It might describe the organization itself, as we did at St Helen's ("to be a caring church") and Trinity ("to be a global center for Christian formation"), or it may describe the desired effect of the organization, as it does at Wycliffe Hall ("to see the nations transformed by the gospel"). Either way, it should generate a sense of excitement, which is one of the features people look for in a leader.[4] The statement should be short enough to be remembered, and significant enough to be inspiring. That is a challenge, but one well worth pursuing.

At Trinity School for Ministry, this last stage of articulating the vision statement was the hardest. We had plenty of good material to work on, but it was a challenge to get it into an agreed statement. This was the stage when I became most involved. Our first attempt was too bland and, thankfully, we got that feedback. There were several revisions and lots of helpful input. When the final statement came out, only one word needed to be changed – "international" became "global" – and it was received with real joy. That was a relief for those of us who had been involved in developing it. Looking back, it was an important milestone. As Steven Croft says of vision clarification, for the leader "there is no deeper challenge."[5]

It is hard to exaggerate the need for prayer and for seeking the Lord's guidance at every point in this process. Vision discernment is a vital stage in the Christian leader's work of taking the people of God on the mission God has given you. It is essential for this task that you do all you can to be following the Lord's direction. The priority is to be seeking God's blessing by doing what God wants you to do. As you seek to articulate that future it needs to be the Lord's own destination you are describing, and not simply what you or others would like to see. However, if all your vision-discernment energies have been directed towards trying to please God, there can be a proper confidence that it is God's own vision that you discern. So, as you undertake the task of vision formation, try to maintain an attitude of dependency on God, humbly expecting the Lord to graciously shine heavenly light on your deliberations, and to reveal a

4. Rob Goffee and Gareth Jones, *Why Should Anyone Be Led by You? What It Takes to Be an Authentic Leader* (Boston: Harvard Business Review Press, 2019), 194. The other qualities that followers look for are authentic leadership, a sense of significance, and feeling part of a community.

5. Steven Croft, *The Gift of Leadership – According to the Scriptures* (Norwich: Canterbury Press, 2016), 3.

description of the future of God's own choosing. Remember Proverbs 3:5–6: "Trust in the LORD with all your heart, and do not rely on your own insight. In all your ways acknowledge him, and he will make straight your paths."

Articulating the Purpose

With the vision statement in place, you need a succinct way to describe the overall activity that could move the congregation or organization towards that vision. This is the purpose statement and it addresses the questions: Why did God call us into existence? What should we be doing to become the church or organization described in the vision statement? United States President John F. Kennedy famously had a vision for space exploration. He called for a mission to be undertaken to send astronauts to the moon and bring them back again safely within a decade. That was a powerfully motivating purpose statement, and it was accomplished. What would a purpose statement look like for your church or organization? It may be less dramatic than that one, but it can still have a wonderfully energizing effect.

The same team that worked on the vision statement might be best suited to writing the purpose statement, building on the work they have already done to describe a hopeful future. Or this could be done with a wider group such as the senior leadership team with the governing council. It is now a matter of shifting the focus to see what activities might help bring the vision about. This is an opportunity for brainstorming possible elements of such a purpose statement, spelling out what could be done to bring the vision into reality. Then it is a matter of allowing time for what the group regards as the most active ingredients to rise to the surface. After that, those elements need to be crafted into a draft purpose statement, which can be offered to others in leadership for their feedback. Finally, it is a matter of further revisions until agreement can be reached. It may come down to one sentence as it did at Trinity. Or it may take two or three as it did at St Helen's.

At Wycliffe Hall, the purpose statement emerged from work on vision and purpose clarification that had been carried out before I arrived. It meant that we had all the ingredients we needed to develop a vision statement and purpose statement at virtually the same time. The vision statement was the harder of the two to clarify, and meant recognizing our role in the wider world more explicitly than we had done previously. Our vision is "to see the nations transformed by the gospel." The purpose statement then spelled out our contribution to that enormous task: "by renewing Christian leaders in prayer, character, preaching and thinking." Our focus is on preparing people for their leadership roles in the worldwide mission of God. That is why we exist. It has proved helpful for us to spell out in more detail how we plan to do that, by stating that "Christ's love compels us to train lifelong disciple makers in community with excellent Bible-centred teaching in a thought-provoking city." Each element of that statement can then also be further expanded to be more specific still, and that has proved helpful in connecting the big-picture vision with the everyday details of what we need to do.

As Rick Warren makes clear in his book *The Purpose Driven Church*, purpose statements can be the driver of a church or organization, with vision in a secondary place. The purpose may well endure after a vision has been fulfilled and a new one is required. The stress is then on what is being done and why, rather than on where you are trying to go. Wycliffe Hall is one of those places where we refer to our purpose statement more frequently than our vision statement. We still value our vision statement, and many have said how much they appreciate it, but it is the purpose that has a stronger role in driving our daily life. It can shape curriculum, help recruit students and staff, and enable us to evaluate how well we are doing. It also keeps reminding us of the purpose of all we do, which, as management expert Simon Sinek has shown, is hugely valuable for a leader in keeping everyone energized and moving forwards.[6] In fact, in some situations, just having a purpose statement, or indeed a vision statement, alongside the core values, may be sufficient.

Capturing Your Core Values

Lastly, there is the matter of describing your core values. These are the values held in highest esteem by your church or organization which help you explain to yourselves and others how you do what you do. It is good to involve as many people as possible in this process. It could be the focus of a retreat day for your leadership team and governing council. You might want to include a few people who are not already directly involved in your church or organization, but who understand and support what you stand for, and may see your values more clearly from their outsider perspective, as they did at Trinity. This too is a brainstorming process in which you prayerfully discern what matters most to you as a church or organization, trying to get that list down to roughly the four to six top items, the ones you care about most. You want to be able to state them clearly and in such a way as to enjoy widespread support. Check them

6. Simon Sinek, *Start with Why: How Great Leaders Inspire Everyone to Take Action* (New York: Penguin, 2009), 185–186.

with as many people as possible before you settle on them to be sure you have captured your core values accurately. As management researchers Jim Collins and Jerry Porras point out, it is vital to remember that "you do not 'create' or 'set' core ideology. You *discover* core ideology."[7]

Once you can state your vision, purpose and core values, you can put them to good use to help bring about that vision, and to draw many people into that purpose and, we trust, into a closer relationship with Christ as a result. Like an archer, you know where you are aiming, why you are doing so, and how you plan to hit the target. Now it is a matter of communicating and implementing it. Andy Stanley of North Point Community Church, Atlanta, USA, has developed a set of tools for "making vision stick": stating it simply, casting the vision constantly, repeating the vision regularly, celebrating the vision systematically, and embracing the vision personally.[8] This approach also applies to the purpose and core values. You want to be living out these commitments, and looking out for stories where the vision, purpose and core values are in evidence. You also need to be willing to challenge behaviour where they are not.[9] Once you have a vision, purpose and core values it is hard to state them too often or to use them too much. They bring so much together into such a sharp focus, and offer clarity to every part of the organization's life. This is a huge benefit to any leader.

Conclusion

Leaders are the keepers of the vision, and those who follow their leadership are being invited into that vision. The overall leader should embody the vision and be its champion, with other leaders actively supporting it, which may sometimes feel like being Aaron or Hur holding up Moses's arms (Exod 17:12). Discerning a vision, and the purpose and core values that accompany it, can be hard and time-consuming work, but it is priceless. It gives you clarity about what you are supposed to be doing, why you are doing it and how you are doing it. It also means you can describe the future into which you are taking people,

7. Jim Collins and Jerry I. Porras, *Built to Last: Successful Habits of Visionary Companies* (New York: HarperCollins, 1994), 228.

8. Andy Stanley, *Making Vision Stick* (Grand Rapids, MI: Zondervan, 2007), 18–54.

9. Ian Parkinson has a very helpful chapter on establishing a healthy culture, which sets out the sequence of modelling, explaining, expositing dysfunction, inviting participation and reinforcing the desired culture, which is summarized in the vision, purpose and core values, but especially the core values. Ian Parkinson, *Understanding Christian Leadership* (London: SCM, 2020), chapter 6.

following the direction of Jesus Christ, in the power of the Holy Spirit. And when you have that vision and work towards it, you know that you have the support of the other leaders and of the wider congregation or organization. It is hard to put a value on that. It enables you to maintain the future orientation which every leader needs.

Taking It Further

How might you grow as a leader in discerning vision, purpose and core values?

1. (a) Write a vision statement for your next holiday, ideally working with someone who will be with you. This should describe what it would be like if it turns out as you hope it will.

(b) Produce a purpose statement for that holiday – that is, why you are going.

(c) List the core values that explain how you want to take that holiday.

2. (a) Write a vision statement for yourself, describing what you want to become a decade or more from now.

(b) Produce a purpose statement for your life.

(c) What values do you hold most passionately?

(d) Combine 2 (a), (b) and (c) onto a single page and put it where you can keep referring to it, perhaps in a prominent place on your computer, or framed on your desk.

3. (a) Write a vision statement for your family, if you have one, describing what you want to become a decade or more from now. Involve other members of the family if you can.

(b) Produce a purpose statement for your family.

(c) What values do you hold most passionately as a family?

(d) Combine 3 (a), (b) and (c) onto a single page and put it where you can keep referring to it as a family, perhaps in a prominent place in your home.

Phase 4

Implement Plans

So, you have established trust, identified leaders and discerned a vision, supported by a purpose statement and core values. The time has now come to implement plans to achieve that vision, the fourth phase of leadership. This is where most leaders spend most of their lives: setting goals and working out plans to achieve them. For that reason it requires the fullest discussion. It is where we become more concrete and ask questions such as, "Where do we want to be this time next year?" and "What should we be doing now in order to see that happen?" This is a wonderful remedy to the malaise leaders often suffer when they feel unable to get to those important things that would really make a difference, because of the day-to-day demands of their job. The plans that stem from your vision, purpose and core values should be prioritized over any other plans, helping you to know when to say "yes," "no" or "later" to requests that may come across your desk. Now that you have the support of the leadership and membership for a shared vision, it is entirely reasonable for you to shape your daily work to promote all possible movement towards it.

There are two particular dangers to be aware of here. The first is that it is quite possible to have relied on God in prayer to get to this point but to become strangely worldly now. You may think, "I can take it from here." But that would be a big mistake. In this phase, as in all the others, the Christian leader is first and foremost a follower of Jesus Christ. The task here, as elsewhere, is to be saying your prayers and seeking God's daily guidance about plans for the future. That is not to say, "Don't make any plans," and nor is it to say, "Make plans and ask God to bless them." It is instead a matter of seeking the Lord's guidance about the future and making plans that are sensitive to what God is doing, which may mean some of those plans will have to change.

There is also the opposite danger. Some leaders find the prospect of implementing plans rather dull and stifling, preferring their time to be more free-flowing rather than working through the stages of a larger project. They want to be responding to the issues of the day, to be meeting people, or to be working on talks and sermons. Implementing plans does require self-discipline, some measure of surrendering personal preferences to work towards a greater good. Hopefully, however, the vision behind these plans has caught your imagination, and you want to see it come about. You will also wish to avoid that sense of frustration people experience when they hear a lot about a vision but see little being done to bring it about. And there is still plenty of time for those aspects of your job you enjoy the most. If these are your challenges, I suggest you read this chapter not expecting to take everything on board, but to be thinking about who might help you put your plans into action, and to look out for those two or three things that might make you a better leader. If you do that and find it really helps, you could always come back to this chapter again at another time and see what two or three other things might help you most then. So use all that follows to improve your leadership and to secure the support you need, rather than treating it as a manual that has to be followed in every detail.

I am also aware that what is described here is the work of several years and can look rather daunting when presented all at once. Do remember that this is an overview. The intention is to help leaders to stand back and see the whole canvas of their work, and get a sense of what might come next.

Implement Plans: A Case Study

When it came to implementing plans at St Helen's Church, Laurence Gamlen was again very helpful. He enabled us to think about the goals we wanted to set and what plans would help us achieve them. Until we had some clarity about what we were trying to accomplish, making plans would have proved very hit or miss. As he memorably put it, the order should be: ready, aim, fire.

Goals and Objectives

Our consultant challenged us to focus on the near term, and to formulate "SMART goals," an idea attributed to Peter Drucker's "management by objectives" concept.[1] The acronym stands for:

1. Peter Drucker, "Management by Objectives and Self-Control," in *The Practice of Management* (New York: Harper & Row, 1954), 105–118. SMART goals are not mentioned there but seem to have emerged organically according to Mike Morrison in "History of SMART

- Specific: something in particular that is worth measuring
- Measurable: something that can be measured
- Achievable: something that is stretching but possible
- Relevant: something that matters
- Time bound: something with a time limit to it

There can be difficulties with this approach, and it is good to be aware of those from the start. Evangelism adviser John Finney, in his *Understanding Leadership*, notes that it is really people rather than organizations that have goals. He also points out that not all goals are measurable or achievable, and that goals are often not achieved, which leads to discouragement.[2] Management consultant Edwards Deming observes that the things you really want to know are things you cannot measure, such as, "How many people would want to be involved with this church or organization if they knew about it?" He is also concerned that goals might be achieved in unhelpful ways so that people hit their targets, but hurt the organization in the process.[3] And Jack Hayford, Pentecostal minister and Chancellor Emeritus of King's University in Los Angeles, USA, argued against goals in "Why I Don't Set Goals."[4] He said that they lead to a performance orientation rather than a prayerful dependence on God, although he acknowledged that when he sought the Lord for the goals, they were very helpful.

I think the difficulty with goal setting lies chiefly in working according to the flesh rather than looking to the Holy Spirit as our guide, to return to the contrast in Galatians 5. If we can discern goals that help coordinate our combined efforts to do what we believe the Lord is leading us to do, I think they can be enormously helpful. We need to remain open to the possibility that we have misunderstood God's leading, and to ensure the goals we set are our servants and not our masters. It is also important that they really are achievable. Sometimes numerical objectives are set that are far too ambitious, so leaders understandably prefer to avoid thinking about them. We also have to remember that this is about kingdom work, not empire building.

Long-term goals for five- or ten-year periods can be useful in describing the church or organization if the vision were fulfilled, in which case they

---

Objectives," https://rapidbi.com/history-of-smart-objectives/, accessed 13th November 2020.

2. John Finney, *Understanding Leadership* (London: Daybreak, 1989), 119–121.

3. See "W. Edwards Deming's 14 Points for Total Quality Management," ASQ, accessed 6 February 2020, www.asq.org/quality-resources/total-quality-management/deming-points.

4. Jack Hayford, "Why I Don't Set Goals," *Christianity Today*, accessed 3 February 2020, https://www.christianitytoday.com/pastors/2007/july-online-only/090905a.html.

are often called "objectives." Leaders can then set intermediate goals as mile markers to enable them to see whether or not they are progressing towards those objectives. In a larger church or organization, these goals might be broken down for different departments and employees so they can see their part in the organization, which can also be very helpful, provided not too much weight is placed upon them.

Such longer-term objectives can also assist the leader in describing the future he or she hopes to see. On one occasion at St Helen's I was sharing my concern that we needed more teachers for our children's work and was very surprised when another leader pointed out that this was the first time she had heard me mention how much this mattered to me. It was one of my top priorities, but I had not said so. I could have avoided that oversight by having established goals and objectives.

At St Helen's, we ended up with four goals and we assigned one to each of the next four years. The goals were:

1. To increase overall attendance at home groups by ten people and to establish a new daytime group within a year's time;
2. To increase the membership to 150 by two years' time;
3. To increase average attendance at Sunday services to 150 children, youth and adults by three years' time;
4. To increase regular financial giving by 9 percent a year over the next four years.

These goals were developed by the Church Council. They were challenging but not overwhelming, because they were based on the numbers from previous years. They helped us to focus on the things we thought would really enable the church to carry out its purpose of growing in our love for God, caring for one another and serving the neighbourhood. They stressed the value of the home groups, church membership and church attendance since these should help the church become more caring and able to reach out, as the vision stated. It included a measure of the level of giving because that was seen as a key indicator of spiritual growth. The goals also gave us numbers we could usefully watch and work towards for the benefit of the church and its mission. We monitored progress towards these goals and discussed them at our council meetings and annual church meetings. Every three years the council would go on a day's retreat and update the whole set of goals. These practices kept the goals regularly before us, and ensured they were revised as necessary. For instance, while we were able to see almost all those goals achieved, it became clear that we could not identify a leader for a daytime home group, so that element was dropped.

Strategies and Tactics

With goals and objectives in place, it was time to make plans to achieve them. What initiatives would we take to reach those goals? Those initiatives, often called strategies, form the major part of a plan for the future. A strategy might be: "To help newcomers become integrated into the life of the church." Each of those strategies then needs to be broken down into actions, sometimes called tactics, which in this case might be appointing someone to oversee the integration of newcomers, who would talk to them and see how they could get more involved in the church if they so wished. Such day-to-day actions help the church carry out its purpose, which is where the leadership rubber hits the road.

The strategic initiatives we developed at St Helen's were to:

1. Recruit more home-group leaders (for goal 1).
2. Look out for regular attenders who could become church members (for goal 2).
3. Consider new ways of introducing people to the church (for goal 3).
4. Recruit a leader for the children's work (for goal 3).
5. Encourage more frequent attendance by those who come occasionally (for goal 3).
6. Work on our annual stewardship programme for a special day of giving: Gift Day (for goal 4).

Each of these strategies had someone assigned to take the lead on it, and to work out more detailed plans for how to go about it. They would often need to involve other people in those plans, which was itself a leadership development opportunity.

The hardest strategy to implement was the fourth one: "Recruit a leader for the children's work." For that, we would need a suitable candidate and the resources to pay him or her, since we were unable to find anyone with the necessary skills who could give the required hours as a volunteer. Finding such a person, and securing the necessary funding, would both be major challenges.

So we prayed. Then we got connected with a youth club on one of the housing estates near St Francis Church which needed two children's workers but could afford to pay for only a few hours, so they didn't think anyone would apply for the positions. However, if their hours were combined with ours, they became viable jobs. But that would mean finding not one but two children's workers with the relevant qualifications and with an active Christian faith. The significant challenge had increased significantly.

We secured financial support for what the children's workers would do for St Helen's Church, and for St Francis Church, which was starting a Sunday afternoon congregation at that time. The money came from neighbouring churches. This was the fruit of relationships that had been built up over several years, and of the awareness that we were working in a particularly challenging part of inner-city London. Churches of very different theological commitments shared a desire to see this ministry happen, and they were willing to support it financially. Then the youth club director persuaded the borough council to pay for the hours worked at the youth club, after some initial reluctance. We were delighted.

Finally, we advertised the position. The deadline for applications passed. No one had applied. It was a great disappointment. That Monday evening, as we prayed together, one of our leaders sensed that she had received a prophecy that God would supply the candidates for this work. The next day, a children's worker came to St Helen's asking if the vacancy had been filled. She and a friend of hers from the same church were looking for such an opening. They both exceeded the qualifications and experience we had specified. They were also committed to the Christian faith. Those two children's workers proved a tremendous blessing to St Helen's, to St Francis, and to the youth club. They were a source of a great deal of joy. And we experienced these joys as a direct result of the apparently routine tasks of implementing plans, showing that such planning can have unexpected benefits.

Even before we had the vision, purpose and goals in place at St Helen's, we had been making plans to address issues as they arose. In one case, our initial strategy floundered and we had to look for another approach. It occurred in our attempt to restart the church plant. We had refurbished St Francis house and Ian Dowsett was living there with his family. They were looking for ways to reopen the derelict St Francis Church building next door. At the same time, we noticed that we had plateaued in attendance numbers at St Helen's. We invited Laurence Gamlen to visit again. He pointed out that we were 80 percent full at our main service on Sunday, which meant newcomers might feel there was no room for them. So it would be a good time to plant a new congregation.

Our architect's initial estimate to revitalize St Francis Church was nearly ten times our annual budget! We did not have that kind of money and could not see where we might find that level of support. Then Sure Start, a government initiative, began, which meant there would be regeneration money available for the public housing development where St Francis Church was. We got together with representatives of the three housing trusts on the Dalgarno Estate, the borough council and the local director of Sure Start, and we met every other week for eighteen months to see if we could put together a children's centre, a preschool service centre, and a worship space in St Francis Church. Exciting plans were drawn up and hopes were high as initial funding promises came in. Then one of the members of the team moved to a new job. As a result, a substantial share of the funding was lost. Things quickly unravelled from there, to everyone's disappointment. The plan did not succeed, despite all the time, effort and prayer invested in it.

At this point, Ian had established a leadership team for the church plant and was looking for somewhere for the new congregation to meet. None of the available local buildings was large enough for it. So we went back to our architect and asked him a very different question: "What would be the minimum we would have to spend in order to reopen the church building?" It was about half our annual budget! The day that estimate came in, Malcolm Colmer, our archdeacon, was visiting. He was responsible for church buildings in this area of London and was keen to see St Francis reopened. When we shared this estimate with him he asked, "How much money do you have?" I explained that we had none. All the money that came into the church went straight out in expenses. He said he would have to check with Bishop Michael and others, but that he was willing to loan us those funds and have us pay them back later. What a joy that was! It meant we could have the church reopened for the summer in readiness for a children's mission. From that mission, the new St Francis congregation was launched. Our initial plan had not worked out, but God evidently had other things in mind. There was a huge amount of rejoicing when this all came together. It was a lesson in seeing that, in the end, it is a matter of following the Lord, and going where the Spirit leads.

There are many times when things do not go according to plan. The popular military quote attributed to Helmuth von Moltke the Elder, "No battle plan ever survives contact with the enemy," has lessons for Christian leaders. Unforeseen challenges and obstacles arise, and it is important to adapt our plans accordingly so that the purpose can be achieved in another way. Here again we see the value of establishing trust and cultivating leaders who can think prayerfully and faithfully, and together discern whether changes of approach are needed in order to bring about the vision.

Implement Plans: The Ingredients

Depending on how you define the terms, making plans may be the moment when a leader becomes a manager. Management skills will have already been deployed before this point, no doubt, but if we understand the leader to be the person who perceives where an organization is, has a vision for where it is to go, and makes plans for how to get there, it is the third element of strategic planning that is most often associated with the role of the manager. In that sense, every leader needs to have some management skills. In particular, leaders are called upon to manage talent (people), treasure (money) and time. Let us outline what this might involve.

Managing People

Managing people is about bringing out their God-given talents to enable them to play their part in the purpose of the church or organization, in accordance with its core values. This perspective helps avoid any sense that time spent with the individuals you manage is time away from your purpose. It is time spent fulfilling that purpose, and perhaps some of the most productive time of all. Managing people well has enormous benefits for everyone. And where those people are Christians, it is an aspect of discipling them, helping them grow into maturity in Christ (Col 1:28).

Before anyone can expect to manage employees or volunteers effectively, he or she must first learn the art of *delegation*. That involves overcoming any initial reservations, such as "By the time I've taught someone else, I could have done it myself," or "They won't do it the way I would do it. I might as well do it myself." That may be true for some tasks, such as "Would you mind giving this message to Mary for me?," but such thinking will quickly defeat any leader who has a significant work to do. Then it is a matter of delegating well by choosing:

- The right person – who has the appropriate knowledge, skills and time;
- The right task – something worth doing, which makes sense as a piece of work to delegate;
- The right way – providing clarity about what you want, when it is due, who can help, what resources are available and what authority he or she has to make decisions.

After that, you need to support the person without interfering, and provide him or her with constructive feedback. Finally, offer thanks to show how much the work was appreciated. This can be done verbally, by email or in writing. A handwritten thank-you note does not take long to write but will be appreciated for a long time afterwards. I have been surprised how often people pin these on a board at work to keep in front of them. Here, as in every aspect of managing people, it is about applying the golden rule: "do to others as you would have them do to you" (Matt 7:12) if you were in their position.

So what are the main features of good people management?

Recruit Carefully

There are few more important decisions a manager makes than in recruiting people. Jim Collins, author of the management classic *Good to Great*, describes this as getting the right people on the bus, which he says is absolutely vital.[5] When you need to recruit someone for a position, whether as an employee or a volunteer, put together a small *recruitment committee* to prayerfully work on a job description and person specification. The job description describes the job itself, listing what needs to be done, and the person specification describes the kind of person who could do the job. That will include the qualifications and experience that would enable someone to do it, making clear what is required and what would be desirable. Often these two documents together are called the "job description" for short.

The *job description* should include your vision, purpose and core values, and be explicit about whether a candidate needs to be sympathetic to them, in which case no faith commitment may be needed, or if the candidate needs to actively support them, probably meaning he or she would need to be a Christian. In some countries this might have legal implications, so it needs to be thought through carefully. It is also important to specify whether this is a full-time or part-time position, and who the person would report to. It is worth taking care to get the job description right, so that it lists all the aspects of the role, and probably includes "other duties as agreed" to allow for unforeseen requirements. Involve several people who understand what the job entails to ensure nothing gets overlooked. That way, potential candidates can see if they might be a fit, and the recruitment committee can discern which candidate might be the best fit. Advertise the vacancy widely and get the word out anywhere you think a potential candidate might be found, making clear the deadline for applications. I have come to see the value of contacting people to alert them to the opening, not to suggest the job is theirs for the taking, but to ask if they know anyone who might be a suitable candidate, or whether it might be of interest to them. There may be good candidates who are not

5. Jim Collins, *Good to Great* (New York: HarperCollins, 2001), 41.

looking for a move, and by reaching out to them it is much more likely they will apply. The application itself could be made by candidates filling in a form designed for this purpose, or by sending their Curriculum Vitae with the contact details of two or three referees, and a cover letter explaining why they think they would be a good match.

When the deadline for applications arrives, assemble the recruitment committee and go through the applicants, sorting them into three piles, "Yes," "Maybe" and "No," according to whether they should be called for interview, being careful to avoid discrimination on the grounds of gender, age, disability, or any other protected characteristic. *Invite three to five candidates for an initial interview.* If there are not enough among the "Yes" candidates, you may need to draw on some of the "Maybe"s. Video conferences or phone calls are helpful for candidates who live far away. This is a good stage to contact the referees to collect their insights. Applicants who are no longer being considered need to be informed promptly and graciously.

At the interview, take time to introduce candidates to the church or organization and help them see what their work would involve. You might want to give them a practical exercise, and a profile questionnaire like the DiSC test. I like to start interviews with prayer, and to be clear that we are seeking the Lord's guidance throughout the search process. Interview questions should be based on the job description, with similar questions going to each candidate for fairness and comparability. Do they have experience that reveals the character and giftedness required for this position? Can they give you examples of when they have done the kinds of things you would want them to do in this role? Allow them to ask you questions too. This all helps to make a good match.

It is always worth taking time to get this right. It may involve more than one interview, especially where the first interview is done remotely. It is better to appoint no one than to employ someone who is a poor fit. As Proverbs 26:10 warns, with a memorable image, "Like an archer who wounds everybody is one who hires a passing fool or drunkard." Human resources consultants like to say: "Hire slowly, fire quickly." Not appointing can be a hard decision to make, and I have only been involved with it a few times, but an unsuitable candidate is unlikely to be happy or effective in the position and, if he or she wants to stay, can be quite problematic. It is also disruptive if that person leaves and another search is required. Better to face the short-term disappointment of re-advertising than pay the longer-term price of a poor appointment.

Once a decision is made, you can offer the job to the successful candidate and see if he or she accepts it, before contacting the others and giving them feedback to help in future interviews, if they wish. A *letter of appointment* with start date, salary, benefits and job description should then be sent to the new employee for the sake of clarity.

This process might be more than you need for recruiting to some *volunteer positions*. Perhaps it could be scaled down for them. But it is still good to have a job description so that volunteers are clear what you are asking them to do, and about who they report to, how long you are hoping they will do it, what resources they have at their disposal and who is available to assist them. This is an aspect of the vital skill of managing expectations. Difficulties often arise precisely because someone thought he or she was expected to do something, when in fact he or she was expected to do something else. That is a road to frustration and disappointment, which is best avoided.

At St Helen's Church, once some of the initial problems had been addressed and home groups were getting established again, the time came to look at how everyone could play their part in the life of the church if they wished to get more involved. We used the Network Course from Willow Creek Community Church, adapted somewhat for a British audience, to help people identify their passions, gifts and readiness for new service. It became a regular part of our annual programme. The first time we ran the course, it had a significant impact on the church, especially for those who found themselves getting involved in new ministries, and having the joy of exercising their God-given gifts in those areas. Others were relieved to be able to step out of roles for which they had come to see themselves unsuited, which was also helpful. New leaders emerged, and some other leaders moved into new roles where they were a better fit, which made a big difference. As I prepared to teach the course, I had to write short job descriptions for all the different roles in the church. I was amazed how many there were. But I do know that having those job descriptions written down proved a benefit to those ministries, and to the people who got involved with them.

If you are a leader in a large church or organization, or have wider responsibility for a denomination or organization, you may have a number of people ready for a move internally, whether as paid employees or volunteers. Jim Collins suggests you put your best people onto the greatest opportunities rather than on the greatest problems.[6] Although every leader needs to be a problem solver and must face challenges as well as opportunities, if you wish to see results for the kingdom of God there may be some wisdom in having your most able leaders on the greatest opportunities, since this is likely to yield the best results. It also means that they are more likely to be encouraged by

---

6. Collins, *Good to Great*, 58.

their work and to grow in their leadership. This might even mean that they eventually outgrow you as a leader. If you can work with them without feeling threatened, so much the better. This is the kind of undefended leadership Simon Walker sees in the most effective leaders.[7]

In all your recruitment work, be sure to comply with all legal requirements and best practices. That may mean involving human resource consultants if you do not have a human resource manager on your team, and in some cases seeking their advice even if you do.

Coach Constantly

Once you have recruited someone, the next task is to see how you can help that person to do a good job, and to pray for him or her regularly. You will, first, want to know what motivates the person, which is likely to be the chance to achieve what is expected of him or her, and to be recognized for doing so. The person is also likely to be motivated by the work itself, and, in many cases, by the opportunity for greater responsibility and advancement. Researchers have found that financial reward is further down the list of factors affecting job satisfaction than we might expect, behind these other features.[8] Second, you will need to spend time finding out his or her strengths, and what activates those strengths, which might well be recognition. And, third, you want to know what learning style will be most helpful: whether that be to analyse information, to see the whole picture, or to learn by experience.[9] This is a reminder that different people need to be managed differently. As the proverb succinctly says, it is "different strokes for different folks."

Managing Individuals

As soon as someone starts in a new role, whether paid or unpaid, it is vital to be clear what you are asking that person to do. This is a key part of *orientation.* People want to know what they are supposed to be doing and how well they are doing it. This sets the tone for future service. The job description is helpful here, and enables you to set the initial priorities by choosing two or three main goals for the year that would make a real difference to the church or

---

7. Simon P. Walker, *Leading out of Who You Are: Discovering the Secret of Undefended Leadership* (Carlisle: Piquant, 2007).

8. Frederick Herzberg, "One More Time: How Do You Motivate Employees?," in Harvard Business Review, *HBR's 10 Must Reads on Managing People* (Boston: Harvard Business Review Press, 2011), 38.

9. Marcus Buckingham, "What Great Managers Do," in Harvard Business Review, *HBR's 10 Must Reads on Managing People*, 103.

organization. Leadership experts Kenneth Blanchard and Spencer Johnson, in *The One Minute Manager*, recommend having goals that can be stated in one minute or less, to be sure they can remain clearly before the employee.[10] Managers should set priorities for those who report to them, but it is wise to involve them in setting these goals since they will know what else is required of them. It also encourages buy-in to those priorities. Progress towards those goals, which might initially include getting to know the organization better, can then be monitored through the year and reviewed annually, with new goals set and training identified.

Depending on their role, you may want to meet the people you *supervise* every week or two, or every month, for half an hour to an hour to see how they are doing in their work and in their wider lives. I like to start a meeting by saying a prayer and then suggest that the person I am meeting says a prayer at the end if I think they would be comfortable doing so. During the meeting, it is good to look at all their main areas of responsibility, allowing the person to raise any issues, to discuss ongoing work, and to keep in mind their annual goals. Such meetings help identify training and support that might be needed, and cultivate a culture of learning. Then it is a matter of allowing the person to do the work. It can be tempting to interfere or take over some project if it is not going well. But this has a debilitating effect. Such micromanagement or more drastic intervention can leave you overwhelmed with tasks, and discourage the employees or volunteers rather than empowering them and building their competence and confidence. The goal is to help them thrive, and to support them in every way you can.

Our ideas of how to supervise others might well be shaped by the experience of supervision we have had ourselves. No doubt that will vary considerably among Christian leaders. I look back with gratitude on those who supervised me in teaching, in the electronics industry, and in the church and theological colleges. These have been largely positive experiences. Not that I wish to replicate everything I have seen, but I have had many excellent role models. If that is not the case for you, it might be helpful to find someone who could act as your work consultant and offer you the experience of being supervised that you could adapt to your own style of supervising others.

With a job description in place and the initial priorities set, it is now a matter of *coaching* for success. Blanchard and Johnson go on to explain the value of giving praise in one minute or less, and sharing reprimands in one

10. Kenneth Blanchard and Spencer Johnson, *The One Minute Manager* (London: Fontana, 1983), 101 (for a summary), or the whole book (it is only short).

minute or less, which provides clarity about what is expected and allows people to get rapid feedback when they do well or badly. It is good to offer *praise* quickly, specifically and generously when things are done well, allowing time for the person to enjoy the moment. And when a *reprimand* is needed, it is best done soon after the event, though not in public, being specific about what was wrong with the person's behaviour and how you feel about it, allowing time for the person to feel the discomfort, and then assuring the person that you want him or her to succeed. All this will help the person grow in the role. People normally hear criticism more loudly than praise and, according to research by Emily Heaphy and Marcial Losada, for every one rebuke you want to issue about six praises.[11] So after a rebuke, it is good to look for a chance to praise the person soon, so he or she does not become discouraged. We want to build up goodwill in every way we can.

It is often easier to learn from praise than it is from rebuke, since it is much simpler to do something right again than it is to make the correct adjustments to something previously done wrongly. Often there are many ways an action could be improved, and it might be that next time the person gets the same thing wrong in a slightly different way. So there is much to be said for focusing on celebrating what someone does right. It is helpful to the person and to those who saw what he or she did, since they learn what kind of action gets praise. This positive reinforcement, associated with behaviourist B. F. Skinner, tends to be especially effective with people who want to please their manager, which employees and volunteers generally do. Kenneth Blanchard captures the idea in the title of one of his leadership books, *Catch People Doing Something Right*. So take every opportunity to thank people and praise them for doing good work.

Similarly, if you want to see some *behaviour change*, it can be more helpful to say, "Please could you do more of [something positive]," rather than, "Please don't do [something negative]." For instance, asking someone to speak more loudly in group settings so everyone hears is likely to be better received than complaining that the person speaks too quietly. Or asking someone to write emails or reports in a particular way rather than complaining they are written poorly. Hopefully, the first of these will come over as an encouragement to the person to share his or her ideas well, whereas the second is a telling-off for expressing them badly, which might leave the person feeling discouraged. In

11. Research conducted by Emily Heaphy and Marcial Losada, cited by Jack Zenger and Joseph Folkman, "Giving Feedback: The Ideal Praise-to-Criticism Ratio," Harvard Business Review, 15 March 2013, accessed 7 September 2015, https://hbr.org/2013/03/the-ideal-praise-to-criticism/.

both cases the same goal might be achieved, but the former approach is likely to be more upbuilding.

For many leaders, a *rebuke* is hard to deliver because it involves conflict. There is also the challenge of determining whether it will have the desired effect or make matters worse. However, there are times when it really is necessary, and then it can help if you rehearse what you plan to say beforehand, remembering to criticize the behaviour and not the person, and to affirm the person in ways you truly can. Where the rebuke has risen to the level of a disciplinary matter, it is important to have someone else with you when you meet, and perhaps suggest that the person being reprimanded brings someone as his or her advocate, in case questions arise later about what was said. In this case, it is important to put key points of the conversation in writing for the sake of clarity and in case you ever need to take the matter further.

If the problem behaviour is so serious that it might involve a *time out from a ministry*, or even a period of exclusion from the organization, you should involve more senior leaders from the denomination or governing council. If there is to be a meeting with this person, it helps to start it in prayer, waiting on the Lord together as needed to be sure this too is a ministry time, albeit a painful one. Allow the person to respond to the concerns you are bringing, and be sure the necessary support or counselling is put in place for him or her as follow-up, getting legal advice as necessary. On the occasions when I have been involved with such interventions, I have been struck by the importance of expressing a genuine desire to see the person do well, to make the needed changes and to be restored to the ministry from which he or she is being excluded. This too has to be an expression of love, not only for those badly affected by this person's behaviour, since you are addressing their concerns, but also for the offending person.

Managing Teams

Managing people can be a major task if you have a large team. It is normally best to have one person manage no more than about five to twelve people, depending on the kind of work they do. So, for a bigger organization, it might be a matter of developing a structure that allows some of those you manage to manage others, and by doing so, learn the skills of management and leadership. In the case of a large church or organization, there may need to be further layers of management. Any such organizational change is complex, and a work consultant can be very helpful in guiding the process, as we found at St Helen's Church.

If you have a team of people working in the same ministry area, it is good to have them *meet together* regularly, perhaps every week or month. This can help foster a sense of community, which is positive for all involved. Teams work best when they have both tasks to do and social interaction that helps them get those tasks done. There is a balance to be struck here, and it will depend on the nature of the organization.[12] But when team members focus on tasks to the detriment of relationships, they will tend to fragment. And when relationships are overstressed, the team may enjoy being together, but not get much done.[13]

One of the striking things about working at Wycliffe Hall is the coffee break at 11 a.m. The whole staff team is invited to this social half hour every working day. Different people come each time, but it is notable that when lots of people are attending, relational challenges reduce, and when few come, they increase. No doubt there are other factors at play here, with the popularity of the gathering reflecting the quality of relationships, and the volume of work to be done. But the value of having this time, especially when we face any challenges or when unhelpful rumours are circulating, is remarkable. It is time well spent.

It is important that *meetings* have an agenda with clear starting and finishing times, and that you try to stick to them. Beginning and ending with prayer makes it clear that the goal here is to follow God's leading in all things. You might also need to stop mid meeting to pray if you think something requires it. Be sure all the main elements of the team's work are on the agenda, and check beforehand, or at the start, if there is anything else team members would like included. If something is likely to come as a shock, or to meet with strong resistance, it might be best to talk with those concerned in advance so that the group conversation can be fruitful, or, when necessary, not to raise the subject at that point.

It is good to have *minutes* taken at the meeting to provide a record of at least the decisions taken and actions decided, and to have them quickly distributed. They should then be reviewed at the start of the next meeting, noticing what follow-up may be needed from actions taken and seeing what

12. See Rob Goffee and Gareth Jones, *The Character of a Corporation: How Your Company's Culture Can Make or Break Your Business*, 2nd ed. (London: Profile, 2003), 22–43. If there is a strong task focus but low sociability, Goffee and Jones call it a "mercenary" culture; if it has strong task focus and high sociability, it is "communal." Where there is a weak task focus and low sociability, it is "fragmented," and if it is weakly task focused but strongly sociable, it is "networked." Each of these demands a different style of leadership.

13. Rob Goffee and Gareth Jones, *Why Should Anyone Be Led by You? What It Takes to Be an Authentic Leader* (Boston: Harvard Business Review Press, 2019), 100.

other actions are required for issues that were not resolved at that meeting. This holds people accountable for what they have agreed to do and gives a clear sense of purpose to the meetings. It is not just meeting for the sake of meeting.

It can be very helpful to "*manage by wandering about*," as William Hewlett and David Packard, founders of Hewlett Packard, termed it,[14] so that all members of the team see you outside the group setting and have an individual connection with you as you visit them in their offices. This is something extroverts like myself naturally warm to, but it may be uncomfortable for introverts. However, even doing this just occasionally allows team members to raise matters that would not seem a good use of the group's time or merit a visit to your office. It gives you the chance to ask questions to understand them and their work better, to encourage initiative, and to celebrate the small wins that can accumulate into the momentum that every leader wants to see.

Group dynamics is a study all of its own, and it is good for leaders to take some time to understand them. One very helpful analysis comes from psychologist Bruce Tuckman.[15] He points out that there tend to be certain stages which groups normally go through: forming, storming, norming, performing, and adjourning. Each stage has its own characteristics:

1. Forming: when team members get to know each other and consider their own role.
2. Storming: when conflict occurs as different expectations and styles of work emerge.
3. Norming: when, and if, conflicts are resolved, and group members settle into their new roles.
4. Performing: when the team focuses on the work it has been given to do.
5. Adjourning: when the team comes to an end because its work is done.

I have found this analysis very helpful, especially when difficulties emerge in a group early on and I cannot see why. Perhaps it is because the group is at the storming stage? It is worth bearing in mind that when members are

---

14. Hewlett Packard's approach is described in many places, including Thomas J. Peters and Robert H. Waterman Jr., *In Search of Excellence: Lessons from America's Best-Run Companies* (New York: Harper & Row, 1982), 122.

15. Bruce Tuckman's model is available in many places, including "Forming, Storming, Norming, and Performing: Understanding the Stages of Team Formation," MindTools, accessed September 2015, https://www.mindtools.com/pages/article/newLDR_86.htm.

added to the group or taken from it, the process restarts, even if on a smaller scale than at first. Tools such as Belbin Team Roles, the Enneagram, the DiSC test, the Myers-Briggs Type Indicator and others can be very helpful here. Not only do they enable us to understand how we and other people prefer to work, but they can also identify who else might be helpful in the group for it to perform better.

Another widely used analysis is that of Patrick M. Lencioni in his *Five Dysfunctions of a Team.*[16] He draws attention to the dangers of the absence of trust, which makes people defensive. Then there is the fear of conflict, which stifles debate. From that follows a lack of commitment, which leads on to the avoidance of accountability, and that ends in inattention to results, which renders the team ineffective. Lencioni's remedy is that the leader should lead by example, being willing to show vulnerability, to encourage debate and conflict, to hold people accountable for what they have been asked to do, and to be clear about the results the team should produce. At root, though, we notice that this is fundamentally a matter of building and sustaining trust, which, as we saw in Phase 1, is foundational to all that a leader does.

Sometimes, tensions emerge between two team members which can make it hard for the team to function well, and some *conflict resolution* is required. On such occasions, it can help to meet with each of those involved to understand what the concerns are and perhaps to suggest ways they can resolve the matter between them. Where that is not successful, you might propose that the two of them meet with you, or some other mutually agreeable mediator. Have one of them express his or her concerns clearly but graciously to the other, without interruption, and then have the other party summarize and reflect back what has just been said, showing that he or she has heard what was said, and checking he or she heard it correctly. Then the process is repeated for the second person to speak and the first person to reflect back. From there it is a matter of agreeing what they might do differently in the future to improve their working relationship. I have seen this process work to good effect, but it does rely on a willingness to have such a conversation, which is likely to be uncomfortable. However, this is a work of peacemaking, which Jesus commends to his disciples (Matt 5:9).

When things go badly in some part of the team's work, seek to learn for the future without trying to assign blame. It is important to encourage people to bring work problems out into the open, and an atmosphere of blame tends to

16. Patrick M. Lencioni, *The Five Dysfunctions of a Team: A Leadership Fable* (San Francisco: Jossey-Bass, 2002).

shut communication down. There will always be mistakes and failures, and it is much better to learn from them than to bury them. If a failure becomes public, having someone skilled in communication becomes especially important. Well-crafted statements that express what was done and why it was done can help to set the record straight. Having a communications manager is immensely helpful at such a time, but in lieu of that, it is probably worth engaging a consultant on these occasions if you can.

Your own relationship with the team and its members also needs to be managed. You cannot simply see yourself as part of the team, because you are its leader, but nor do you want to be so distant from it as to appear aloof. It is a challenge for someone to move from being a part of a group to being its leader, as I did at Trinity School for Ministry. You will no longer be seen in the same light by them, and you must learn to see yourself differently too so you can have enough emotional distance that you can make the right decision for the team even when it might be unpopular for one or more of them. But nor should you avoid informal social occasions when you are invited. The team members need to feel a personal connection with you, which they value. Egyptian Christian businessman Khaled Bichara was noted for the way he worked hard to build up teams and to stay close to them, even when he became nationally and internationally famous for his work. He recognized the value of those relationships and he invested himself in them.

There is no doubt that building teams is a challenge all of its own. But it is worthwhile on many levels, not only in terms of the development of team members, but also for the sake of the work you can do together. A study by Patrick Laughlin and a team of researchers at the University of Illinois at Urbana-Champaign found that groups of three, four and five people repeatedly outperformed the best individuals in solving problems. Laughlin attributes this to the greater ability of people to generate and adopt correct responses when they work together.[17] This is evidence that working as a team produces better outcomes than do individuals working alone. Once people see this happen a few times, even those who prefer to work on their own may be won round to such teamwork.

There are two particular aspects of leading a team, or groups of teams, which we have touched on but deserve special attention before we move on: managing change and managing communications.

17. Patrick R. Laughlin, Erin C. Hatch, Jonathan S. Silver and Lee Boh, "Groups Perform Better Than the Best Individuals on Letters-to-Numbers Problems: Effects of Group Size," *Journal of Personality and Social Psychology* 90, no. 4 (2006): 644–651.

Managing Change

Managing change is a necessary skill for every leader, because if the church or organization is to achieve its vision, everything cannot stay the same: some things will have to change. When leading these changes, it is important to take people with you, as far as possible. So managing people is not just about maintaining the status quo, it is also about helping them move through change. Knowing how to lead such change successfully is therefore vital to the work of leadership.

The first thing the leader needs to have in place is the *process for making such changes.*[18] That requires two main elements: the people with the recognized leadership authority to make changes, and an agreed plan within which those changes can be understood. This is where the work on leadership development and vision formation can really pay dividends. It is important that there is a recognized *leadership team* in place which has oversight of such changes. At St Helen's Church, that was the Ministry Leadership Team. At Trinity School for Ministry it was the Cabinet, involving the Principal, the Deans of Academics, Advancement and Administration, and the Dean of Students. At Wycliffe Hall it is the Senior Management Team, which consists of the Principal, Vice-Principal, Finance Director, Dean of Women and Director of Ministry. These leaders have the privilege of working out how to bring about strategic change towards the vision. They have the crucial role of setting organizational priorities, in consultation with their governing council.

To make changes well, the leadership team will want a framework for decision-making, drawing together the vision, purpose, core values and the plans to implement them into a single document, a *strategic plan*, or mission action plan, as some churches prefer to call it. This might typically include:

- Introduction: a brief history of the church or organization
- Vision: plus purpose and core values
- Analysis: strengths, weaknesses, opportunities, and threats facing the church or organization
- Objectives: numerical and other goals describing the vision in more detail
- Strategies: initiatives that should help achieve the vision
- Tactics: what needs to be done to carry out the strategies

18. John Kotter, *Leading Change* (Boston: Harvard Business Review, 2012), 23, offers an eight-stage process for managing change which is worth consulting for a more detailed analysis.

- Next Steps: how the strategic plan is to be communicated, used, monitored and updated

The Introduction should be quite straightforward to put together by someone with a knowledge of the history of the organization. And we have already considered how to develop the Vision, the purpose statement and the core values. The Analysis can be done by the leadership team, with input from the council and other stakeholders to help provide honesty and clarity about the current situation. It is a matter of listing the main strengths and weaknesses of the organization, and the main opportunities and threats it faces. The Objectives make the vision more concrete by describing in more detail where you are hoping to be in five or ten years' time. This normally includes specifying key numbers, such as how many people you anticipate being involved with the church or organization, the staffing required, and the finances needed to make it a reality. If there is little appetite for such numerical goals, listing two or three things you would like to see happen in the coming years would be helpful in guiding what activities would be most advantageous, and make them more likely to happen.

The Strategies lay out the initiatives that you believe would help make the journey to the vision, and they may vary considerably in number, from the few we had at St Helen's to the many we have at Wycliffe Hall. Where there is a large number of strategies which might be implemented over the five- to ten-year time horizon or beyond, the priorities for each year need to be set regularly by the leadership team. At Wycliffe Hall, the Senior Management Team does that on an annual retreat, after a review of progress on the strategic priorities for the previous year. When this is combined with budgeting resources to support those priorities, or setting fundraising goals for them, that can be very helpful indeed.

The Tactics could be listed here too if there are only a few strategies. But where there are many strategies, it may make more sense not to include the tactics but to say that they are being worked out separately by those responsible for implementation. It is interesting to note that some people tend to be more comfortable thinking about strategies, while others prefer to work on the tactics to implement them. Spelling out who is to do what and when, using SMART goals, will focus these efforts. Often this is a case of making implicit goals more explicit, as well as setting fresh goals. It might also include a Big Hairy Audacious Goal (BHAG), as James Collins and Jerry Porras recommend in *Built to Last*, such as planting a thousand churches in five years, as Archbishop Bob Duncan called the Anglican Church of North America to do in 2012. The

Next Steps then explain how this plan will be implemented and carried forward, to be sure it brings about the intended benefits and realizes the vision. It might be decided at this point that the organization itself needs to be restructured to support the strategic plan.[19]

As strategic priorities are discerned, decisions can then be made about what to change and how to change it. Leaders are *making decisions* and *solving problems* all the time, of course, but there is probably more at stake here because of the scale of what is being decided, so it can be helpful to agree a deliberate set of steps to follow. Here is one approach:

1. Collect the decision-makers:
   - Is this something you can decide alone?
   - Do you need advice from others?
   - What team of people might together bring about the best-informed decision?
2. Pray:
   - Take time to seek the Lord's wisdom and be attentive to the Spirit's promptings.
3. Clarify your objectives in terms of what you are trying to achieve:
   - What would you like to see in this situation so that it ties into your overall vision?
   - If you have conflicting objectives, you may need to weight them for relative importance.
4. State the problem or opportunity:
   - Describe how the current situation falls short of the desired one.
   - This should be in one sentence per problem, or per opportunity, to be sure it is really clear.
5. List the alternative possibilities to address the problem or opportunity:
   - Brainstorm possible options; no idea should be ignored or dismissed at this point.
   - What steps could you take to arrive at the situation you desire?
   - It may become obvious that more information is needed before a decision can be made.

19. Ian Parkinson has a very helpful diagram that shows how all the elements of a strategic plan are interrelated, for which he acknowledges his debt to James Lawrence. Ian Parkinson, *Understanding Christian Leadership* (London: SCM, 2020), 228.

6. Evaluate the alternatives and choose the best option(s):
   - List the pros and cons for each major option.
   - Think how to optimize the decision to maximize the pros and minimize the cons.
   - You might consider starting with a small-scale pilot to test an idea, or having a trial period.
7. Act on the decision:
   - Pray and put in place the steps needed to implement the decision.
   - Communicate the decision widely, with the reasons for doing it.
   - Monitor the outcomes of the decision, and learn from it for the future.

This approach to decision-taking was developed from a number of widely available ones while I was at Trinity School for Ministry, and we used it many times. When we wanted to address problems in the leadership of corporate worship in chapel, a challenge faced by many Christian leaders, I called together those involved in our chapel life: the Director of Chapel, the lecturer in Preaching, and two Pastoral Theology lecturers. We prayed, and then described our objectives – what we would like to see happening – and agreed that we all wanted to produce outstanding service leaders who knew, loved and honoured the tradition of Anglican worship. Then we were able to state the problem in terms of how we fell short: there was a general sloppiness in some of our officiants. After that we brainstormed a number of possible improvements, such as having faculty and staff model how to officiate for the first week or two of the academic year, and having student groups take responsibility for leading a week of services at a time. Then these and other ideas were evaluated and some of them implemented, including the two listed above, through conversation with the faculty and wider community. This proved a great help to our corporate worship.

An example of the benefits of a *trial period* for managing change occurred while I was leading St Helen's Church. I was taking a closer look at some of the furniture one day when I came across a large wooden table off to one side of the building, covered up under a brightly coloured cloth. I removed the cover and saw that the table had been hand carved for the church, matching some of its arches, and bearing a plaque commemorating the founding minister of the church. It seemed to be a much more suitable communion table than the one we were using regularly, which was disconcertingly tall. I asked others about it and discovered that it had been considered as the communion table before, but there were a couple of people who strongly preferred the current arrangement.

There were some other items of church furniture, including the pulpit and lectern, which seemed to be in the wrong place. They were all easy to move, so, as an experiment, some of us swopped over the tables, and moved the pulpit and lectern to what seemed more suitable positions. Anyone who came into church that afternoon was asked what he or she thought of this layout. They all preferred it. Then one of the two people I had heard would be against such a change came in. She was pleasantly surprised, but not in a hurry to see such a change.

That evening, we had a Church Council meeting. After taking advice from other leaders, I decided to leave the furniture in its new temporary place and have the council members come in and see what they thought. There was a lot of warmth about the new arrangement. We decided to keep it that way for Sunday and explain to the congregations that we were trying this as an experimental arrangement for the next six months. If after that people preferred how it had been previously, we would put the furniture back. They have remained in those places ever since.

Where possible, those who will be affected by a change should be engaged in the process of working out the change, which is known as "*shared governance.*" In any such discussions, do be clear when you are sharing information, when you are asking for advice, and when you are wanting a decision, to avoid confusion about what kind of input you are requesting. Not only does such consultation bring collective wisdom to the changes being made, it also helps generate buy-in for those changes. As the old proverb has it, "People are down on what they are not up on." Even if people do not have their ideas accepted, they at least know that they were heard. It is also better to have such feedback before a change is made rather than afterwards, by which time unnecessary mistakes might have been made. Here again, the establishment of trust and the cultivation of leaders prove highly valuable, as do the agreed vision, purpose and core values.

Once the leadership team has decided something needs to change, it is important to *communicate clearly* why the change is needed, what the likely timescales are and how it will benefit people, acknowledging that such change causes people stress. According to the French chemist Le Chatelier, all change is opposed, and what is true of chemical systems is also true in human societies. So don't take it personally when change meets resistance. People instinctively worry about what change might mean for them, since they cannot know its impact, and that is unsettling. Some adapt to change quickly, many adjust to change more slowly, and some are highly resistant to any change.[20] So as you communicate about the changes, encourage people, tell them stories of successes along the way, and continue to love people however they respond.

In order to manage change well, leaders need to learn how to *negotiate* with individuals and groups, since disagreement and conflict are inevitable. When such situations arise, remember that the goal of a good negotiation is an arrangement that works for everyone. It is not about winning or losing but about working together for a shared goal. Then agree on the process for the negotiation: Who will be involved? When will they meet? When is a decision needed? It is important to be clear about what the parties really need as opposed to what they would like but could actually do without.[21] There may well need to be some give and take in these conversations, and the decision-making process laid out above might prove helpful. But hopefully, by God's grace, you can arrive at an agreement, which then needs to be clearly stated and communicated. If all goes well, good negotiations should enrich the relationships between those involved.

Sometimes, the strength of *opposition* to change is very great. For instance, I was hoping to change the pattern of Sunday services at St Helen's to have Holy Communion more often. I had worked hard to make these services welcoming to those not yet committed to the Christian faith and thought I was suggesting a pattern of services that would be acceptable to everyone. However, a significant number of key people, most of whom were highly influential but not in senior leadership in the church, strongly opposed the change. They made it clear that they, and others, would leave the church if the changes went ahead. I met them individually to talk the issue through, but couldn't persuade them of the benefits of making these changes. Eventually, I came to the conclusion that it would be best to leave the services as they were. Perhaps we could have returned to the idea a few years later, but that did not occur during my tenure.

On other occasions, it seemed right to press ahead with a change despite strong opposition and threats to leave the church. One such case was the change of the timing of the first service on Sundays at St Helen's, moving it from 9:30 to 9:15 a.m. to allow longer at the end of the service for fellowship before the next service began. It would primarily benefit those who came to that earlier service, but it did inconvenience them by asking them to arrive sooner. There

---

20. See Alan J. Roxburgh and Fred Romanuk, *The Missional Leader: Equipping Your Church to Reach a Changing World* (San Francisco: Jossey-Bass, 2006), 103.

21. See Roger Fisher and William Ury with Bruce Patton, *Getting to Yes: Negotiating Agreement without Giving In*, 2nd ed. (New York: Penguin, 1991).

was some opposition, but the most vocal resistance came from two members of the congregation. I met with them, listened to them, and talked the changes through with them. Their opposition remained, but we went ahead with the change of timing. I am glad to report that those who opposed the change did not leave the church, as I feared they might.

Probably the biggest single decision we made at St Helen's was about the redevelopment of the church hall. Large sums of money were involved and the decision would commit us to the Montessori school for at least twenty-five years. No one on the Church Council was used to making decisions on that scale. They were understandably afraid. Following advice from one of my leadership mentors, on the day we had to make the final decision I invited everyone in turn to share their thoughts before we went to a vote. It was clear that many felt this was too big a commitment and they were inclined to vote against it. My turn to speak came last. Seeing what was likely to happen, I spoke about the great ministry opportunities this relationship would open up with the school and others in the community. I also shared my fears about declining the offer. How could we expect other churches nearby to go on subsidizing us, knowing that we had turned down such an amazing opportunity? In the end, the proposal was agreed with only a couple of votes against. In time, those who opposed the agreement came to see that it had been a good decision. But that was a stressful season of decision-making.

Managing change well is crucial to a leader's work. So too is managing communications. How are we to handle communications well?

Managing Communications

Communication within the church or organization, and with the wider public, is a vital aspect of leadership. It is essential that people internally know what is going on and feel part of something bigger than themselves. Regular emails, newsletters and, in some cases, magazines can be very helpful in this regard. Communication externally helps establish a profile and a reputation. It is good to seek every opportunity to spread the news about what God is doing. Even apparently small initiatives can make a big difference. I was amazed to see the impact it had when we put up a new name board outside St Helen's Church. The old one was falling down and the new one which replaced it had been attractively designed by a member of the congregation who did that work for a living. It broadcast its positive message day and night, and changed the perception of the church in the neighbourhood.

Making effective use of *social media and the website*, and building relationships with journalists, can all pay dividends. Someone needs to be responsible for overseeing all this, with a strategy that shows who you wish to communicate with, what you want to communicate, and how and when you plan to do so. It is important to regularly communicate your vision, purpose and values. You can also maximize the use of your talks and writing by sharing them, or parts of them, more widely. It is rare indeed to find any organization where its people think they get too much communication.

I did not have many opportunities to engage with *journalists* at St Helen's Church, and only twice spoke with the press as an assistant minister at St John's, Hyde Park – once when we had an event for horse riders and I was asked whether horses had souls, and a second time when a reporter for *The Times* newspaper phoned to ask me to list the Ten Commandments, presumably to show that not all church leaders could. I think I got all ten, though I do wonder if I used one of them twice! In Pittsburgh, a journalist from a Christian radio station contacted me one day with a question about Reformation Sunday, which I engaged with over the phone. From that interview a relationship developed that became a regular monthly interview. It was a joy to have to think of topics to address and to work out how to approach them. I was also pleased at the way it raised the profile of the college in the area and attracted people to us. It prepared me for a more challenging interview with the BBC World Service about the appointment of Archbishop Justin Welby, where issues over human sexuality were raised. Wonderfully, I was given the last word and had the privilege of sharing the gospel message in the final minute of the interview.

When the opportunity arises for an *interview with a reporter*, either because of an initiative on your part in sending him or her a press release, or in response to a local or national news event about which the reporter thinks you might have something to say, start off by finding out what is wanted:

- What is the subject the reporter wishes to discuss?
- What sort of audience is it?
- How long will the interview or report be?
- And if this is for the radio and television: Is the show live? If so, what will the first question be?

When the reporter wants an interview right away, it is wise to ask for time to get your thoughts together and to offer to phone back in half an hour or so. Then prepare what you wish to say by collecting your ideas into a few main points with notes, not a script, including illustrations, anecdotes and examples. Anticipate the who, what, where, when and why questions that might arise. Get people praying for you.

For a *face-to-face interview*, be sure you are dressed professionally, and listen carefully to the questions. Smile, give good eye contact, and remain relaxed. Speak factually, frankly, deliberately and to the point, in a firm but friendly manner. Remember, you know more on the subject than the interviewer. Try to establish a conversational style which is lively, brief, simple and jargon-free. Be courteous and gracious, and avoid cutting in, unless you feel you must, in which case do it confidently. Don't rush in to fill silences, and be willing to say, "I don't know." Avoid a simple "yes", "no" or "no comment," and never get angry. Make sure you say what you wish to say and avoid going "off the record." This is a great opportunity, and you want to make the most of it for kingdom purposes.

Say "Farewell" Well

At some point people step down or move on and it is important to *express appreciation* and thanks for the work they have done. This is the right thing to do for its own sake, but it also communicates an important message to those who continue to work in the church or organization: you are appreciated and the work you do matters. This becomes difficult if someone has been asked to leave, for which great care must be taken and professional advice sought, but even then it is good to bring that time to an end in the best way possible. Before anyone leaves, it is helpful to have an exit interview to get the person's feedback on the strengths and weaknesses of the organization at that point. He or she may have valuable thoughts about the church or organization and its future, and feel unusually free to share them at such a time.

There can be an understandable *tendency to hold on to your best people* when they indicate they may be looking for a move. And it may indeed be that there are changes you can and should make to keep them longer. But sometimes it is right for them to leave and you are left wondering: How will I cope without them? Who could take their place? This can indeed be a test of faith. We had a wonderfully gifted young leader arrive at St Helen's soon after I started. He was mature in the faith, experienced in youth work and keen to promote the gospel. We met up soon after he arrived and looked at possible ways for him to get involved. Shortly after that, he was gone. In this case, it wasn't so much that we had let him go to some other role, but that his job had taken him away. That was a hard blow at the time. Years later, after I had left St Helen's, we met up again and he told me how he had become more involved in the life of the church once his work circumstances changed. By then he was preparing for ordination, and he could see how his time at St Helen's had helped get him ready for that.

Knowing that people will leave at some point is a reminder of the importance of *succession planning*. Where can you look to find leaders who could step into the roles currently filled when the present incumbents move on? Here too job descriptions can be helpful. Identifying and developing potential leaders is also very significant. Openings will arise and you want people ready for them when they do. Where possible, it is good to appoint people from within the church or organization, since they understand the culture and what you are trying to do. However, for paid positions, even if you do expect to appoint from within, it can still be helpful to advertise to be sure you have the best person for the job. This is not only for the benefit of the church or organization, but also for the sake of the person appointed, who knows that he or she was not the only candidate. So you may wish to build up a database of where to advertise for different positions when vacancies do arise.

This management of people is the first and foremost management task of any leader, and it has many parts to it. But it does not stand alone. There is also a need to manage money and to manage time. Let us turn next to the management of money.

Managing Money

In order to see a vision realized, leaders must gather the financial resources required to achieve it and manage those resources well. That will include both the ways in which money is collected and how it is invested, whether in people or in buildings and equipment. Human beings have been given the immense privilege and responsibility of stewarding God's resources (Gen 1:28), and leaders have the power to decide how that is done not just for themselves, but also for others. So money needs to be spent wisely and effectively, and our financial management must be above reproach (2 Cor 8:20). How are we to do all this?

Become a Joyful Fundraiser

For some leaders, revenues flow in because they are selling products or services. Other leaders, however, rely on voluntary support. Leaders of Christian organizations generally find themselves in the latter category. So, to some extent or another, they need to be fundraisers, even if it is only to include taking a collection in a service or meeting. Often it needs to go a lot further than that.

The apostle Paul was a fundraiser, seeking support for the church in Judea (2 Cor 8:1–15). He makes clear that the first goal of fundraising is for people to *give themselves to the Lord* (v. 5). Realizing that we belong to God, both because we are the creatures of God and because we are the redeemed creatures of God, is where Christian fundraising must begin. Calling ourselves and others to give themselves to God as living sacrifices (Rom 12:1) is primary here as it is in all other aspects of Christian ministry.

There also needs to be a recognition that *everything we have was given us by God*. As the psalmist reminds us, everything belongs to the Lord (Ps 24:1), and as James says, all good gifts are God's gifts (Jas 1:17). So God has a call not only on our lives, but also on our possessions, including our money. Giving generously, sacrificially and joyfully (2 Cor 8:2–3; 9:7) is therefore a spiritual activity, and one that is a vital part of discipleship. We want to encourage that in our churches and organizations. I support the idea that Christians should give a tithe, 10 percent, of their income to the local church, or perhaps split between their church and other ministries. Beyond this, I encourage people to give other offerings as they are able. Whatever approach we take, leaders need to seek financial support for their church or organization, and to communicate their needs graciously and winsomely.

Jesus spoke about money often, but many Christian leaders are *uncomfortable talking about money*, since it seems so self-serving, and we fear it might damage relationships with the people we lead. It helps if we are aware of the spiritual importance of seeing all we have as belonging to God, and of the value our resources have for serving kingdom purposes. Martin Luther is said to have remarked that there are three conversions: the conversion of the head, the conversion of the heart, and the conversion of the purse. It can take some time for what we know of the gospel in our minds to truly captivate our hearts, and further time again before we see ourselves and our resources in the light of it. That is a helpful reminder of how significant becoming generous givers is for many Christians. A commitment to generous giving is often a significant step on a spiritual journey.

Henri Nouwen, a Dutch Catholic priest and writer, captures this well in his book *A Spirituality of Fundraising*:

> In [treating] fundraising as ministry, we are inviting people into a new way of relating to their resources. By giving people a spiritual vision, we want them to experience that they will in fact benefit by making their resources available to us. We truly believe that if their gift is good only for us who receive, it is not fundraising in the spiritual sense. Fundraising from the point of view of the gospel says to people: "I will take your money and invest it in this vision only if it is good for your spiritual journey, only if it is good

> for your spiritual health." In other words, we are calling them to an experience of conversion: "You won't become poorer, you will become richer by giving." We can confidently declare with the Apostle Paul: "You will be enriched in every way for your great generosity" (2 Cor 9:11).[22]

So regular teaching on giving not only helps strengthen the finances of the church or organization; it also helps people discover the joy of giving. I hope it might also turn leaders who are reluctant fundraisers into enthusiastic ones, especially as they see the fruit it bears. That is what happened for me at Trinity School for Ministry.

Jesus and his disciples were themselves supported by the generosity of others: "The twelve were with him, as well as some women who had been cured of evil spirits and infirmities: Mary, called Magdalene, from whom seven demons had gone out, and Joanna, the wife of Herod's steward Chuza, and Susanna, and many others, who provided for them out of their resources" (Luke 8:1–3). And although the apostle Paul did not take money from the church at Corinth (2 Cor 11:7–15), he did receive funds from believers in Philippi and elsewhere (Phil 4:15–16; 2 Cor 11:8–9) to supplement what he earned from making tents (Acts 18:3), and had hospitality from Priscilla and Aquila (Acts 18:1–3) and Lydia (Acts 16:15). He also described Phoebe as a "patron" (Rom 16:2, ESV). There have been a number of notable stories of such Christian patronage in the history of the church, such as Humphrey Monmouth funding William Tyndale's Bible translation, Lady Huntingdon supporting George Whitefield's evangelistic campaigns, and John Thornton underwriting John Newton's ministry and hymn writing, including the first publication of "Amazing Grace."[23] Where such a connection can be made for gospel ministry, involving not just financial support but wisdom and prayer support too, it can be truly transformative.

Having some method in place to raise funds for the *routine costs* of the organization, such as salaries, building costs and utilities, needs to be considered. What would be the best way to ask for that kind of support? It might be announcements at gatherings, letters, emails or personal conversations. At St Helen's Church, we developed something I had learned as an assistant minister at St John's, Hyde Park: having annual teaching on the importance of proportionate and sacrificial giving. That might be a short series of sermons on

---

22. Henri Nouwen, *A Spirituality of Fundraising* (Nashville: Upper Room Books, 2010), 19.

23. John Rinehart, *Gospel Patrons: People Whose Generosity Changed the World* (Fullerton, CA: Reclaimed Publishing, 2013).

the topic, with testimonies and supportive printed material about the church's finances and future needs. Here too the church's vision and purpose statements prove helpful. It is a matter of finding what works in your context.

Sometimes the leader is involved in asking for *specific resources* to achieve particular elements of the vision. This might be for one item or for a collection of needs as part of a fundraising campaign, in which case it is wise to engage a fundraising consultant who can help you through such a process. The consultant can assess whether you are in a position to undertake such a campaign, enquire with major donors about their potential support for it, and identify which elements of a campaign are most likely to find funding. He or she can also point you to trusts and foundations worth approaching. After that, the consultant can guide you at every stage of the process. This is invaluable advice that pays for itself many times over. It will generally involve producing a case for support, digitally or in print, setting out the vision and what is needed to achieve it, together with providing financial reports and other relevant information.

Some leaders fear that such fundraising involves pressuring people to give what they would rather not give. However, that is not, or should not be, the case (2 Cor 9:7). It is about building genuine relationships with people who share the values of your church or organization and want to see it thrive. Next it involves finding out what they would love to support, and matching their desire with your need. Then a leader should prayerfully present them with an opportunity to be a partner in this gospel ministry.

When it comes to a *fundraising ask*, the leader's task is to pray, to make a sacrificial gift himself or herself, and then to go to people and present the case for support. Explain what difference a gift would make, and then say, "Would you [and your spouse] prayerfully consider making a gift to help us achieve this vision?" Then it is a matter of being quiet to give them time to respond. Here again you can pray for the Holy Spirit to be at work. A donor may want to know how much you are hoping he or she will give, so it might be good to have a number in mind. Whatever people decide to give – and they may need time to think it over – thank them for it and give praise to God, the giver of all good gifts. It amazes me how many donors have told me they often don't get thanked for a gift. That is poor manners and likely to make them hesitate to give again, quite understandably. So do be sure to acknowledge any gifts, probably with a personal note or phone call, and ensure the money is spent as agreed and not on something else. That way, ongoing relationships are built, and smaller gifts may be followed by larger ones.

One of the great delights of Christian leadership is to see the joy on the faces of those who make a gift to a mission they care passionately about. It became clear we needed to significantly increase our financial support for students at Trinity School for Ministry. I was sharing that news with our governing council when one of the members was clearly moved by the concern. The Holy Spirit seemed to come upon her, and she held her head in her hands. After the meeting, a colleague and I met her in my office and asked her for a substantial gift for scholarships. She said she would give half of that amount, and directed some of it to be used for regular funds. But the scholarship money was not to be used to set up an endowment, from which we could only draw a small percentage. It was to be spent as needed. That amazing gift started a fund to which many others contributed. From that day onwards we were able to offer full-tuition scholarships to all students who needed them. What a blessing it was to those students! And what a joy for that donor, who was virtually skipping as she left my office! As Jesus said, "it is more blessed to give than to receive" (Acts 20:35).

Alf Stanway left his home in Australia to minister for thirty-five years in East Africa with the Church Missionary Society. He served as bishop of Central Tanganyika, where he oversaw a great number of churches being planted, and schools and hospitals being established. He went on to be the founding principal of Trinity School for Ministry. He used to say, "God pays for what he orders," as he led the college in prayers for its weekly financial needs. He would also remind everyone that, by relying on God's provision, the college would be "sensitive to God's displeasure." If it looked as if there would be a funding shortfall, he would invite everyone to ask what God was saying. Did there need to be repentance for anything, corporately or individually? These two principles of fundraising went into the very DNA of the college.

There are many marvellous stories of God providing for Trinity School for Ministry over its lifetime. One of my favourite stories is of the time when we discerned an urgent need for reliable, high-quality educational material for all age groups in the church. The possibility then arose to have an educational centre relocate to Trinity. It would come with a name, but no people. The council agreed that we should pursue it, so we began to look for a director. One of my faculty colleagues thought of someone who had just the right qualifications and experience, including time in the publishing industry. He was about to sign a contract with another college and we had to move fast to draw up a job description, find the funding for the first two years, and interview him for the job. We discovered a foundation that we believed would make a significant gift for it and moved ahead on that basis. In the end, that foundation was not able to support us, which was a disappointment. But just a few weeks later, an unexpected gift came in for almost the same amount of money! Praise God!

The need to find long-term funding for this position played a significant part in deciding to undertake a fundraising campaign. During that campaign, another foundation was identified that might have an interest in this ministry. One of the trustees of that foundation knew the new director of the education centre, and had all sorts of links with Trinity, some of which only become evident when we met. This foundation was able to make a gift large enough to endow the position for the long term! How wonderful it is to see God provide in such remarkable ways.

Have Good Financial Procedures in Place

Christian leaders need to handle money in a transparent and open way, while avoiding sharing confidential information. Having a good *treasurer or finance manager* to help with all this is a wonderful gift. Larger churches or organizations may need someone with suitable financial qualifications, while smaller ones may only need a volunteer who is good with domestic finances. This person will need to oversee any payroll issues, and whatever endowments and restricted gifts there may be. Financial skills alone, however, are not enough. He or she also needs to be recognized as a leader in the church or organization, and to share a desire to see the vision realized, which is a lot to ask of one person. Someone like this can be hard to find in some contexts, as was the case at St Helen's. It might be necessary to pay someone else to prepare the accounts, and to have the treasurer work with that person on behalf of the organization or church.

Proper procedures should be in place for dealing with financial transactions, having at least two people involved in handling cash and ensuring that someone in addition to the treasurer or finance manager reviews bank statements. There should also be regular financial audits. This is to minimize the possibility of the misappropriation of funds, and to protect the reputations of those involved with the money, and of the organization itself. That way, people can be confident that money is being used properly to advance the stated purpose. If the treasurer or finance manager is resistant to these measures, do spend time listening to those concerns and explaining why these steps are needed. If that is not sufficient to resolve the matter, the issue is too important to be left, and may result in you needing to find someone else for the position. This may take courage to do, but it is better to act at this point than to face the much greater difficulties of dealing with the fallout if money is being misappropriated, and trying to restore trust after that.

Careful *budgeting*, prayerful allocation of resources, and regular monitoring of incomes and expenditures are all important. The goal is for the mission to shape the budget, rather than the budget determining the mission, as often happens. There is a danger of being driven by the question "What can we afford?" rather than "What does the Lord want us to do?" With careful stewardship in place, together with prayerful dependence on God for provision of our needs, we may remember the insight of Hudson Taylor, missionary to China: "God's work done in God's way will never lack God's supply."

For the governing council to fulfil their responsibilities, *financial reports* should be presented to them each time they meet, and in a way that can be readily understood even by those without financial expertise. Two main reports are needed. The first is the *balance sheet*, normally an annual listing of all the different assets and liabilities. This shows what is *owned*, which may include buildings, equipment, investments, cash, money awaited from debtors, and so on, and what is *owed*, such as money due to creditors. A strong balance sheet shows considerably more owned than owed, and sufficient assets that can be liquidated into cash if necessary. So the balance sheet gives a snapshot of the overall financial health of the organization. In some cases, it may have very little on it, especially where there are no buildings. In others, there may be a great deal, accumulated over many years. Our task is to manage what God has entrusted to us.

The second financial report is the *income statement*. This is the main financial management tool, and helps those in leadership plan ahead and make adjustments as necessary. My preference is for an income statement that is no more than one page long, so that you can see all the main numbers at once, with a format like that shown in figure 5.1.

With this format, council members need only be able to do basic maths in order to feel well briefed about the finances. It is the second column that is most valuable for management purposes because it shows whether the year is likely to end in deficit or surplus on the current course. It incorporates any significant changes that have happened since the budget was agreed (though it is not a redoing of the budget, and the updates must be kept manageable), and offers a more accurate projection of the main incomes and costs. That reforecast shows where the numbers are above or below what was anticipated in that budget line, and allows the council to pray, and to seek other incomes and savings to avoid a deficit, unless this has been approved for some good reason. The comments column then adds some colour to the raw numbers, such as "a legacy gift was received," or "urgent heating repairs." As the financial year draws to a close, it is this middle column that can then provide the basis of the budget for the following year, once you have incorporated the spending priorities demanded by the strategic plan. We found this approach very helpful at St Helen's Church and at Trinity School for Ministry, and we use something similar at Wycliffe Hall.

Figure 5.1

	Year to date	**Reforecast for the year**	**Budget for the year**	**Comments**
Income				
Largest source	60,225	120,100	130,100	
Second largest	25,318	55,250	45,250	
Third largest	4,005	10,010	9,215	
. . .				
Total income	**89,548**	**185,360**	**184,565**	
Expenses				
Largest category	80,215	160,315	170,195	
Second largest	8,010	15,220	10,215	
Third largest	4,128	6,058	4,155	
. . .				
Total expenses	**92,353**	**181,593**	**184,565**	
Net surplus/(deficit)	**(2,805)**	**3,767**	**0**	

Sometimes major savings are required, especially during a *recession*. We had to reduce the budget by 20 percent over two years at Trinity School for Ministry after a financial downtown, which was a painful thing to do. It included some job cuts. But such actions may be necessary to preserve an organization for the long run.

It can be helpful to develop this income statement beyond one year when you are heading into a *period of substantial change*. For instance, it could be extended to three, five or more years by making reasonable estimates about inflation and so on. When St Helen's Church was about to redevelop St Francis Church and house, we could foresee some substantial expenses, and forecast significant new income streams once we were renting rooms out. These would extend well beyond the one-year time horizon, and by having a five-year income statement we were able to see that in the coming years a new, more stable situation was likely to develop. Expected deficits in the earlier years would be covered by surpluses in later years. It meant that when the archdeacon, Malcolm Colmer, asked how much money we could put into the redevelopment project at St Francis, we could show him we had done our sums and make clear that we really did need help.

There is another key element in financial management, *cash flow*, which is about ensuring you have enough money available to pay bills when they are due. This is generally handled by the treasurer or finance manager, and rarely comes to the attention of other leaders unless there is a concern that financial obligations might not be met. Under such circumstances, it is important to see what steps can be taken to pay what is owed on time.

For many leaders, financial issues are a source of concern, and sometimes even profound *anxiety*, often most acutely in the middle of the night. There were many testing times when I was leading Trinity School for Ministry, especially in my first three years. One of the hardest challenges was facing the financial anxiety when money did not seem to be coming in and we were predicting a substantial shortfall. How would we pay everyone and meet our other obligations? What would all this do for the reputation of the college and our witness to the world? I shared these concerns with others, we prayed, and God provided, but not before we realized that unless those prayers were answered, we were in trouble.

It can be tempting to avoid taking on certain challenges for fear of the financial implications. Careful consideration must indeed be given to the cost of any such project. Jesus warned against starting to build a tower and finding you cannot afford to complete it (Luke 14:28). We do not want to lead any organization into a financial hole. But all leaders need to be willing to *take appropriate risks*. When we are sure God is calling us to do something, it is vital to go ahead and do it. We are to seek first God's kingdom (Matt 6:33). This is why spiritual discernment is so significant to Christian leadership, and that often comes from the senior leadership team in consultation with others, including the governing council.

So we have briefly considered how leaders manage people and money. The next question is how leaders can best manage time.

Managing Time

Leaders must also manage time well: their own and other people's. This is often a matter of leading by example. Leaders need to develop a good balance of work and rest that allows them to find a sustainable pace. This means setting aside enough time for daily Bible reading and prayer, for family and friends, for recreation, and for sleep. It means eating properly and getting enough exercise. It means taking a day off each week for the Sabbath and having holidays for refreshment, bearing in mind that sometimes a day off will need to move to another day to accommodate events you have to attend. I also recommend taking a study day regularly, perhaps each week or month, or at least every quarter, that allows you to keep your mind sharp and to be on top of the material you need to read to be an effective leader. Good leaders tend to be good readers. All this should help you cope with the stresses of leadership and protect against burnout, which afflicts too many leaders.

Managing Your Time

Some leaders find their days largely taken up with obligations over which they have little say. For instance, in rural settings in India, people arrive to see a leader without appointments. However, we want to make the most of the time over which we do have control. Good time management means using the working day well, seeing what needs to be accomplished that day and what may be left until later in the week or another time. I have found it useful to go through the outstanding actions at the end of the week and to write a "*To Do List*," or simply collect the papers and files needing attention into a "To Do Pile," with urgent matters on top to get the priority they demand. That way, I can arrive in the office on Monday morning and start work on the things I most urgently need to do. I try to spend a few minutes preparing brief agendas for the people I will meet, so I know what I need to cover and am not relying on remembering it at the time. This is a great stress reliever and reduces the number of times I disappoint someone by forgetting something significant. I also allocate time in the calendar to important work which may not be urgent but will significantly improve the church or organization. That may be for larger projects, such as developing a strategic plan or preparing for a mission, which need to be broken down into smaller steps. It helps considerably to set dates for each of those steps, or at least for the first step in order to see what else will be involved. Matters that are neither urgent nor important should be left, at least for now.

This prioritizing of what is most necessary may mean that you spend less time doing what you most enjoy, which is one of the sacrifices of leadership, as we have seen. Sometimes the pressure of many urgent matters means you cannot do them all as well as you could if you had more time, and this too might need to be accepted, at least for a while. It is another aspect of self-control and the price leaders might have to pay. But it is important not to be overwhelmed by all that needs doing, and that you are energized by what you do, so some balance must be found.

Once in a while it can be helpful to see how you actually use your time, by *making a time chart* to see how each half hour is spent, and seeing if that time usage matches your priorities. At St Helen's, I discovered the value of having a "To Do Later" list, since that allowed me to keep track of things that I could not attend to at that point but wanted to get to in the longer term. This was very helpful to me when I was repeatedly pressed to get a new hot water supply installed in one of the bathrooms, and could say, "I have a note of that and hope to get to it soon, but we cannot do it right now."

The making of a strategic plan with agreed goals for the year helps you *establish priorities* among all the many things that might have a call on your time. The hope is that your desire to see the purpose carried out and vision realized means that you will want to do what it takes for that to happen. One way of containing the demands of email and other correspondence, which constantly press upon us, squeezing our discretionary time, is to give them attention twice a day, perhaps first thing in the morning and again after lunch, and keeping replies as brief as possible without being curt. Leaders' time should be guarded for long-term fruitfulness, ensuring that they are giving time to what they alone can do because of their leadership role, and delegating other work where possible.

Another time-management tool is to have a sense of the *shape of a typical week*, like that shown from my time at St Helen's Church in figure 5.2 on the following page. Here "Admin" includes all paperwork, emails, meeting preparation and course development, so it is being used in a very broad sense. I would try to take an hour and a half for lunch, plus half-hour breaks morning and afternoon for coffee and tea breaks, though not always successfully. There was Morning Prayer 8:45–9:00 a.m. and Evening Prayer 5:00–5:15 p.m., Monday to Friday. I also had 5:30 p.m. to 8:00 p.m. with my family, since evening meetings tended to start at 8:00 p.m. in London, so I was available for dinner and for the children's bath and bedtime. I booked a monthly quiet day to give me time to clear my head and listen to God, and went to a seminar at King's College, London, about once a month for my studies, if time permitted. I also took an annual retreat and attended a conference each year.

It was important for me to recognize the value of such patterns and to gently but firmly maintain boundaries for everybody's sake. I also found that it helped not to fill the calendar too full, to allow for pastoral needs when they arose. Other leaders will have a schedule that looks very different from this, not least because taking Saturday off is unusual for church leaders. It was only possible for me because there were so few weddings at St Helen's, rarely more than one a year. Whatever the pattern may be, however, having some pattern for your working week can be very useful.

Figure 5.2

	Morning	Afternoon	Evening
Sunday	Services	Start sermon prep; make hospital visits	Admin (sorting out my papers for the coming week)
Monday	Admin	Admin and visits	Service Planning Team or Ministry Leadership Team
Tuesday	Staff meeting	Visits or meetings	Meeting (or on Thursday)
Wednesday	Writing the sermon	Visits or meetings	Meeting or teaching at home (so Cathy could go to a home group)
Thursday	Admin	Visits or meetings	Home (or meeting if not on Tuesday)
Friday	Study	Study	Off
Saturday	Off	Off	Prepare to give the sermon, to revise and learn it

As a church or organization grows, it quickly gets to the point where administrative support is needed so that those with administrative gifts can do the administrative tasks needed for the smooth running of the organization. Leaders can then focus on the work for which they are called and gifted. Not having such support in place may well mean they are spending time doing things for which they are not well suited, or are having to deal with the fallout from things being overlooked and people being hurt as a consequence. So, as the budget allows, I highly recommend bringing in administrative support, even if it is only part-time.

Managing the Church or Organization's Calendar

Leaders need to manage not only their own time, but also the time of the church or organization. When it came to the church calendar at St Helen's, we were able to develop something I had begun to learn as an assistant minister at St John's, Hyde Park: having a pattern for the year (see figure 5.3).This allowed us to spend periods of time focusing on different aspects of the church's ministry, which some church growth experts term "call" (evangelism), "train" (discipleship) and "send" (mission).

Figure 5.3

Emphasis	Preaching focus	Teaching focus
Early September: Children's Mission and Evangelistic Weekend		
Call	Introductory and Evangelistic	Alpha Course, Start Course or Christianity Explored
Christmas		
Train	Discipleship	Membership class Gift assessment and deployment course Lent teaching evenings Stewardship campaign for annual giving
Easter		
Send	Mission to the world	Confirmation preparation classes "How to share your faith" course World mission events Christian Aid week
July: Confirmation, or a Celebration or Festival		

The church year was strongly influenced by the school year, since newcomers tended to join us in September, and we began the yearly cycle with a focus on *evangelism*. There was a mission at the start of the school year with a Holiday Bible Club for children ending with a guest service on the Sunday. We involved children who had been at the Holiday Bible Club in the service, and included testimonies from some of those who were confirmed the previous July. Then we would launch the Alpha Course or another introduction to Christianity for enquirers, from which new home groups might emerge.

The sermons over those months were geared primarily towards seekers and newcomers to the Christian faith, and I would offer a call to commitment to Jesus Christ every month or so at guest services, as well as at the Christmas services. This might involve calling people to come to the front for prayer, kneel at the foot of a cross, or join in a prayer of repentance, seeing me afterwards to receive follow-up material. More recently, I have often invited people to make their response, or to renew that commitment, by raising a hand to their chest at the communion rail when everyone comes forward, or by going to a prayer station. There someone will pray with them: "May you know the forgiveness of all your sins, be filled with the Holy Spirit, and follow Jesus faithfully all the days of your life." This allows such calls to commitment to become a normal part of church life, and has proved helpful to many.

In the New Year, we would shift the focus onto *discipleship*, not only for those new to the faith but for all levels of spiritual maturity. During this time, we ran a membership class for newcomers, with a short history of the church, the vision and purpose, and suggestions about how to get more involved. We also offered a gift assessment class based on the Network Course from Willow Creek Community Church, to help people discover how they might best serve in the church and in the world. We held classes on Wednesday evenings in Lent about Christian living, and ran our stewardship campaign for annual giving in this period, seeing it as an integral part of discipleship.

After Easter, the focus would move to *world mission*, paying special attention to that theme in the preaching, running evening classes on how to share your faith, supporting Christian Aid week, and holding events with mission partners whenever possible. The year drew to a climax with the annual confirmation service. For denominations that do not have confirmation, a celebration or festival day, perhaps including a visiting speaker, baptisms and testimonies, might work well instead. The confirmation preparation classes for youth and for adults at St Helen's tended to be the main place where people came to explicit faith in Christ. Towards the end of the course, candidates would fill in a form to provide details for the confirmation certificates, which included the statement, "I want to be confirmed because . . ." There was a tick box underneath with the option for what they wrote there to be included in the service sheet, since congregations like to know that information, and because it was a form of witness. Then, at the confirmation rehearsal, I would invite people to read out what they had written. Often, once one person agreed to do so, everybody did, which made for a wonderful time of testimony in the service.

The date for the confirmation service was set for July to correspond with the end of the school year, and we had a party afterwards with a barbecue, live music and children's entertainment to make it a day to remember. That might also be a good time for a church or organization to hold a celebration or festival.

This calendar for the year meant that, even as a small- to middle-sized congregation, we were able to do a lot of different things without trying to do them all at once. Here too, this pattern will not suit every setting, but having some kind of pattern like this might be worth considering for any church or organization if you don't already have one.

Conclusion

Making plans and carrying them out is about seeing management as the stewardship of God's resources to bring about God's vision for the church. It is where most leaders spend most of their time. It is the day-to-day work of leadership. Doing these things well is demanding and time consuming, and there is much wisdom in keeping things as simple as possible. Even small simplifications accumulate and are generally worth doing. If something does not need to be done, it may be better not to do it, so that energy is not diverted from more important matters. Implementing plans like this is full of challenges and opportunities, and sometimes disappointments, but it supplies wonderful joys. It is all about the practical steps of taking the people of God on the mission of God, at the direction of the Son of God in the power of the Spirit of God, which is a privilege indeed.

Taking It Further

How might you grow as a leader in making and implementing plans?

1. What skills might you need to develop to be a good manager of people? For example:

(a) Delegation

(b) Hiring people, and bringing their employment to an end when necessary

(c) Annual reviews, including setting goals for the year

(d) Coaching, including giving praise and rebukes

(e) Negotiation

(f) Conflict resolution

(g) Decision-making and problem-solving
(h) Understanding group dynamics
(i) Chairing meetings
(j) Managing change
(k) Managing communications
(l) Managing the media
(m) Making a strategic plan
(n) Implementing a strategic plan

2. What skills might you need to develop to be a good manager of money? For example:

(a) Fundraising
(b) Budgeting
(c) Financial management

3. What skills might you need to develop to be a good manager of time? For example:

(a) Personal time management
(b) Managing the cycles of the year
(c) Managing projects and events

Phase 5

Transition Out

The fifth phase of leadership is transitioning out. There comes a time when the leader moves to another position or retires. All that work of establishing trust, cultivating leaders, discerning vision and implementing plans has, we hope, made a wonderful difference to the church or organization where that leader has served, and it is time for someone else to take it forwards. Since the role of a leader, especially an overall leader, is vital for any organization, it is important that this transitioning out is handled well. No one wants his or her good work to be undone. Instead, we want to make ready for another leader who can take the church or organization into its next chapter.

Transitioning out well is hard to do. There may be a temptation to leave too soon, perhaps because of the challenges faced in the early stages as leaders try to establish trust. There is also the temptation to leave too late, perhaps because of a reluctance to start all over again in a new leadership role. Then there is the issue of how to leave well even if it is at the right time and for the right reasons. When should you tell someone you are thinking of moving on? How should it be announced when you do? What can be put in place to help the church or organization through the transition? How can this time be used to build up and not to tear down? Because these are complex issues, it can be helpful to think about them in advance, and be ready to prayerfully seek the wisdom of mentors who know us and our places of service if we believe it might be time for a move.

Transition Out: A Case Study

I nearly left St Helen's Church a year too soon. I had been asked to serve for at least four years, so when I met two major setbacks in my fifth year – the collapse of our initial plan for the reopening of St Francis Church and concerns about schooling for our daughters – I thought my time might be up. I also had Ian Dowsett for one more year, who could cover the leadership gap after my departure while the search for my successor was undertaken. So I wrote to Bishop Michael suggesting it was time for a move, and he wrote back advising me to stay longer. I am so glad he did. In that next year many remarkable things happened: St Francis Church plant got restarted, our refurbished church hall was opened, and the two children's workers began their work. It would have been awfully sad if I had left after year five and not seen the answered prayers of year six.

At Trinity School for Ministry I was encouraged to continue the work for as long as I did by colleagues, the governing council and outside visitors. That played an important part in discerning whether I really was doing what God wanted me to do. One Tanzanian bishop, Alpha Mohamed, had a particularly powerful impact on me in saying, "Stay longer, stay longer, stay longer" when I had thought my time was nearly up before it was. Again, I am glad I stayed on. During the following years we started an online master's degree, published educational materials, and completed a fundraising campaign for a media centre and studio, student scholarships, sabbatical funding for international scholars, and for a diploma for Hispanic ministers. That was a huge amount of encouragement, and it strengthened Trinity School for Ministry considerably.

The decision to leave Trinity began as we approached the end of the fundraising campaign and Cathy and I were praying about when we should return to England. What might be a good moment for a move for the schooling of one of our daughters would be bad for the other. How would this all work out? One day, out of the blue, our older daughter said she would like to attend university in England. Our younger daughter then began to say that she wanted to finish her schooling in England and go to university there too. Cathy and I began a season of discernment, asking whether it was the right time to move. Mentors both in the USA and the UK affirmed that it might be that time. I learned during these conversations that Bishop Alf Stanway used to say that a leader should leave when things had reached a peak and were going well. That was helpful for me to hear. I had also come to believe it would be good for a new leader to take Trinity School for Ministry into the next era.

Over the years, I have had many conversations with Christian leaders in which I have found it not unusual for leaders to seek a move after three to five years. I even came across a church in the USA that had never been able to keep a leader more than five years although the church was many decades old. I heard about it from the person who was its then leader, and the congregation was convinced he would do the same, however much he assured them he wouldn't. I met that leader some years later and was pleased to hear that he had broken the mould. It is often a bad idea for an overall leader to go so soon. Those first few years normally involve battles to establish the leadership role with those who would challenge your authority. If you leave then, you may well face the same battles at another church or organization, and you could end up spending many years in that difficult phase of establishing trust. You are in danger of missing out on the fruitful years of ministry that come afterwards.

The longer you stay, the more clearly you will be seen as the leader. It is also better for the congregation or organization not to be in transition too often and having to get adjusted to another new leader. So, unless you have become a serious problem for the congregation or ministry, or the challenges ahead really do require a different leader, it is generally wise to push through and keep going despite itchy feet, and stay longer.

Transition Out: The Ingredients

There are many examples in the Bible of people transitioning out of their leadership positions, some for positive reasons and others not. We may think of Moses, whose leadership of the people of God through such an amazing journey of faith came to a sudden halt after he disobeyed God's instructions and struck a rock that God told him to speak to (Num 20:1–12). Because of this disobedience, he was not allowed to enter the promised land to which he had led the Israelites. That task was to be entrusted to his assistant, Joshua. King Saul later failed to fully carry out God's judgement on the Amalekites and tried to hide what he had done from the prophet Samuel. As a result, God rejected him as king and had Samuel anoint David as king in his place (1 Sam 15 and 16).

More positively, we have the example of Jesus preparing his disciples for his imminent death, resurrection and ascension into heaven in John 14–17. He explained more about himself, about the role of the coming Holy Spirit, about the challenges that lay ahead, and about what they needed to do as church leaders. The apostle Paul also prepared churches for his death, writing to give them instructions about their work, with particular guidance for leaders like Timothy who would now be operating without Paul as his mentor (2 Tim).

Discerning When to Leave

In some contexts, the decision to leave lies with someone else, where there may be a pattern of moving leaders on after a particular number of years. If, however, the decision lies with you, then transitioning out requires discernment to know when it is time to move on, or to move others on if you have such oversight. This should not be about a leader giving up, but about sensing when the work in that place is done. There is no formula for this. Research by Christian statistician Bob Jackson in *Hope for the Church* suggests that church leaders are most effective between their seventh and thirteenth years in a ministry.[1] But that is simply to show what typically happens. There are many wonderful cases of people serving for thirty or more years and seeing great fruitfulness. They remained fresh and engaged, making the necessary adjustments in leadership style along the way.

If you are able to *stay and serve well* as the leader in one place, that will have an enormous impact and make good use of all the relationships of trust you build up, and the leaders you develop. It will also mean the vision you discern and the plans you implement can have the maximum effect. This may involve weathering many storms and declining exciting alternatives, but, as John Guest says, "There is a price to pay in leadership to do anything significant."[2] Leading for the long term, and not just as a step to something else, has a lot to be said for it. Leaders need to be able to persevere.

In order to stay the course and not leave too soon, before their work is done, leaders must develop *resilience*. How are they to cope with the disappointments, criticisms and setbacks along the way? As Henry and Richard Blackaby point out, "being criticised, second-guessed, and having one's motives questioned are unpleasant but inevitable aspects of leadership."[3] Research has been carried out into the question of how to endure all these challenges. The main findings are that leaders should respond to such events by keeping things in perspective rather than imagining the worst, doing what they can to improve the situation rather than seeking someone to blame for it, and drawing strength from networks of support rather than becoming isolated.[4] When I faced that very discouraging week at St Helen's Church that meant we were facing a shortfall of two-thirds of the annual budget, it took me several weeks to recover from it emotionally. It was the networks of support that proved the most helpful

1. Bob Jackson, *Hope for the Church: Contemporary Strategies for Growth* (London: Church House, 2002), 160.

2. This was part of a personal conversation.

3. Henry and Richard Blackaby, *Spiritual Leadership*, rev. ed. (Nashville: Broadman & Holman, 2011), 331.

4. Martin E. P. Seligman, "Building Resilience," in Harvard Business Review, *HBR's 10 Must Reads on Mental Toughness* (Boston: Harvard Business Review Press, 2018), 32–35.

to me at that time. I also prayed a lot and kept reminding myself to cast my anxieties upon the Lord (1 Pet 5:7).

Ajith Fernando, who was national director of Youth for Christ in Sri Lanka for thirty-five years, points out how costly the call to service in Christian leadership can be:

> God has called each of us to serve in different places, and there is no such thing as an easy situation for a disciple of Christ. But I think it is sad to see such a large number of Christians leaving situations of obvious conflict and hardship. Christians are people who can stay on in such situations because they are not afraid to groan. This is part of our theology. Because we groan with the joyful anticipation of glory, we are willing to live with frustration when our calling includes that.[5]

Moving for the sake of avoiding pain is unlikely to be a good reason for a transition. We need to stay in the place where God has called us to be and find the necessary resources to stay there until the time comes for a calling somewhere else.

On the other hand, it is possible to *stay too long*. There may come a time when you are no longer the right leader for a church or organization. This seems to have been the case with King Hezekiah, who was commended for his righteous rule in his first fourteen years (2 Kgs 18:5–6). However, when God granted him fifteen additional years following divine healing from a life-threatening illness, things went badly wrong (2 Kgs 20). Some people are aware that they have lost their enthusiasm for leadership or are finding that it has become routine. It might also be a season for a different leader. Management professor Edgar H. Schein suggests that different stages in an organization's life need different leadership styles. At the initial, creating stage, the organization needs an animator; at the building stage, a builder; at the maintaining stage, a sustainer; and at the changing or evolving stage, when renewal is needed, a change agent is required.[6] If no change agent emerges at that crucial point, there is a danger that decline will set in.[7] These stages may be led by one person who

5. Ajith Fernando, *An Authentic Servant: The Marks of a Spiritual Leader*, 2nd ed. (Leyland: 10publishing, 2007), 4.

6. Edgar H. Schein, "Leadership and Organizational Culture," in Frances Hesselbein, Marshall Goldsmith and Richard Beckhard, eds., *The Leaders of the Future* (San Francisco: Jossey-Bass, 1996), 59–69.

7. Management studies reveal that the life cycle of an organization is often like a bell-shaped curve, known as the Adizes Life Cycle. It begins with exciting growth, rises to a peak at maturity, then, unless leaders bring renewal, there is a steady decline towards death. Typically,

can stay for a long time, such as a church planter who goes on to build up the church over many years or decades and supplies the kind of leadership needed at each point. But it may be that other leaders are needed. If your leadership style no longer meets the needs of your present ministry, and you cannot adjust to what is required, it might be right to look for another call.

Leaders whose natural style is to initiate, however, do not necessarily have to keep moving to new positions. They can continue to serve well in one church over many years by starting new ministries where they are. Leith Anderson, President of the National Association of Evangelicals, was senior pastor of Wooddale Church in Eden Prairie, Minnesota, USA, for thirty-four years. He described himself as a starter and not a sustainer. By launching something new every year and building leaders to maintain the different ministries, he was able to stay for the long run. This might suggest ideas for other initiators.

An American bishop who visited Trinity School for Ministry said that after seven years as the leader of a particular church he asked his leadership team every year, "Am I still the right person to lead this church? Do I have the right skill set? Am I helping to take it forward, or is it time for somebody else?" These are great questions, and having people around you who can honestly answer them will greatly assist you with discerning when to leave.

It is possible to stay too long through fear that there will be no suitable successor for us, but this underestimates the providential care of our heavenly Father who, as we see throughout Scripture, delights to raise up leaders. If this concern is holding us back from a move, it is good to be aware of a study of leadership by Howard Gardner which found that "sooner or later, nearly all leaders outreach themselves and end up undermining their causes."[8] He goes on to say, rather strikingly, "Indeed, the greater the accomplishment of the leaders, the greater the strain on the milieu, strong accomplishments breed strong reactions, and by and large, only those effective leaders who die at a young age are spared the disheartening sight of their accomplishments being severely challenged, if not wholly undone."[9] When the Lord calls us into a new ministry, we may trust that God will provide the leader required for the position we are vacating, rather than stay on in that position out of fear.

Another possibility is that you *receive a call* even though you are not looking for one. Then it is a matter of prayer and seeking godly counsel as to whether this is something that might be of God. It could be clear that it is not

---

the length of this process is somewhere around forty years.

8. Quoted in Blackaby, *Spiritual Leadership*, 343.

9. Quoted in Blackaby, 343.

the right time or the right position and you can simply say "no." On the other hand, it may be something you need to explore further. By allowing your name to go forward, while being open about your reservations, you have longer to discern whether this might be the next call for you.

If you have a *family*, an important piece of discerning a potential call is asking whether it makes sense for your spouse and children. Taking their needs seriously and remembering that you are called first to marriage and then to ministry is important. Praying together and seeking the Lord's guidance for the family is a vital part of any transition, not only for evaluating a possible call, but also for the strength of your marriage and the discipleship of your children. Sometimes the changing needs of your family may themselves necessitate a move. If the Lord provides a new call which accommodates these needs, it is a good indication that the time might be right for you to conclude the current work.

Leaving Well

Once you have determined that it is time for a move, the next step is to prepare for the transition. A change of leadership is always a major event, since so much depends on the leader. So you want to plan this well. The first step is to *tell the people responsible for appointing your successor*, if that can be done without the word getting out too soon. This might be a denominational leader or the chair of the governing council, who can start preparations for a search, ideally six to nine months in advance. I was able to do this when I was leaving Trinity School for Ministry, so a search could be started well in advance. These senior leaders need to be informed about such thinking, and may seek to talk you out of it, as Bishop Michael initially did with me. It is also a reminder that they don't like to be caught by surprise, and appreciate being kept informed.

In some situations, it is possible to have a say in your own succession. Where that is possible, it offers the benefit of knowing that the candidate should fit the culture and embrace the vision of the church or organization. If you can identify such a person, and other key leaders share that view, check if the person is open to considering it, and, if so, take the idea to those who have responsibility for making the appointment.[10] If this person does end up being the chosen candidate, the transition still needs to be worked out carefully so everyone is clear about what is happening and when, to minimize confusion. However, if this approach is not possible, you could still be helpful to those

10. See Ian Parkinson, *Enabling Succession* (Cambridge: Grove Books, 2017).

seeking your successor. You may have suggestions of networks worth pursuing or people to approach. The strategic plan should also assist them, since it sets out the vision, purpose and core values of the church or organization, and potential candidates might be invited to express their views about them. This too should help shorten the time taken before a new appointment is made, which can help maintain momentum.[11]

Second, you want to be thinking about having a *transitional leadership team* in place. This will both keep you energized to the end and pave the way for your successor. In some situations, there is an interim leader who will be responsible for the church or organization during the search for the next leader. This may be a member of staff or someone brought in for this season. But even in those cases, it can be a great help to have an established leadership team to help smooth out this transition. At St Helen's, that was the Ministry Leadership Team, and at Trinity, it was the Cabinet.

The transitional leadership team will have an important role in reviewing the vision, purpose and core values, as they draw up a profile of the church or organization for which a new leader is being sought, and a description of what kind of leader they are seeking. That should be a reminder that this is a time not only of sadness, but also for re-evaluation and anticipation. They will play an important role too in oversight during this transitional time. For instance, people may offer to step into leadership roles who might not previously have felt able to do so. That was certainly the case before I arrived at St Helen's, and good things came from that. The leadership team should remember, however, that not all such volunteers have the knowledge, skills and character required for leadership, so their offers of assistance need to be evaluated before they are accepted. As they await the arrival of the new leader there will no doubt be many other matters to address, which will probably keep the transitional leadership team busy.

Third, you might want to *prepare notes for your successor* to help him or her get orientated. My predecessor did this for me at St Helen's and it was very helpful. He also offered to talk with me about the church. It is an offer I did not take up at the time, but later wished I had. Anything you can do to help your successor settle in well will conserve the momentum built up under your leadership. If you have developed a strategic plan, that will be a huge help to him or her. Anything you can provide to give a sense of history,

11. Bob Jackson has shown how many people are lost from churches during longer vacancies, and stresses the need for trying to make a new appointment within six months. Bob Jackson, *The Road to Growth: Towards a Thriving Church* (London: Church House, 2005), 129.

the current situation and any future plans will help your successor get off to a running start. The notes I left for my successor at St Helen's had a list of things I was thinking of doing next, including increasing administrative support, introducing a relationship counsellor, and developing more mission links. If I wrote that document now, I would add running a leadership development course and offering an addiction recovery ministry. Such information is not intended to dictate what the next leader should do. It is, instead, to suggest possible ideas, and where they seem suitable the new leader can say that his or her predecessor was thinking of doing the same, which might be helpful.

The fourth thing you will have to do is *make the announcement* that you are leaving. One or two months beforehand is probably about right for most church and ministry positions, although something more like six to nine months might be better in the case of a role of wider oversight in a denomination or organization. Whoever you report to would be best placed to guide you on timings. It should not be too early or you may become a lame-duck leader, but it should not be too late either or there may be insufficient time for proper goodbyes. It is good practice to let your key leaders know before the announcement goes public so they are not blindsided by it. They might well be offended to hear it when everyone else does, or simply to learn about your departure through the grapevine. Try to tell them just before the public announcement, to reduce the risk of the news leaking out.

Then *say "farewell" well.* This is a chance to express appreciation and thanksgiving for all the good things that have happened, to offer apologies and gain reconciliation where necessary, and to seek and offer God's blessing. It can help to have a letter of resignation prepared so that when you come to share the news in what can be a very emotional moment, you have the words you wish to say in front of you. It was certainly helpful to me when my time came to leave Trinity School for Ministry, as it enabled me to say what I wanted to say at that point. It can also help in crafting an announcement about your departure for your website, social media, ministry email list and press release, if that is needed.

When you are saying goodbye, work on the assumption that you will meet everyone again, so leave each of these relationships in good order. Maybe one day you will work with them in another setting, or need them to give you a reference. You can look forward to seeing them again in heaven and in the new heavens and new earth, if not before. It also models to others how to bring good closure to a relationship.

Any such departure involves an experience of *bereavement* for you, and for those you are leaving. So it is wise to expect many grieving processes to be underway in the following months. Elisabeth Kübler-Ross, founder of the hospice movement, famously identified the stages of grief as denial, anger, bargaining, depression and, finally, acceptance. So don't be surprised if people act out of character during this time, or if problems arise that have not previously surfaced. Be aware of this for yourself, your family and friends, and for members of the congregation or organization, so that you can process the grief appropriately.

This would be a good time to *preach and teach on leadership transitions* if you are in a preaching and teaching role, and to help people not only with their sense of loss, but also to see the opportunities that lie ahead. They need to know that the work of every human leader comes to an end at some point. It is a good time to remind everyone of the main things that you were trying to do during your tenure, to acknowledge your failures, and to perhaps express some regrets. There should be a shared sense of gratitude for the journey which you have undertaken together, and a growing anticipation of the next journey with your successor.

Then, when you have left, it helps if you publicly and privately *offer your successor your blessing* and support, and it is very important not to interfere. You have developed many deep relationships, so do not be surprised if someone contacts you to say, "The new leader is suggesting we do [. . .]; what do you think?" It is no longer really any of your business. You would not have wanted your predecessor to have become embroiled in such conversations when you first arrived in the role, and it is important that you honour your successor in the same way. This does not mean you have to cut off all relationships. You may even visit the church or organization again with the permission of the new leader. I have been back to St Helen's for two funerals, one of which I was asked to lead. But it does mean you should not get drawn into the ongoing leadership issues there. That may be a hard thing to do, especially if you were there a long time, but it is vital for the future health of the church or organization.

Transitioning out, as we have seen, involves discerning the time for such a move, preparing the church or organization for the transition, and announcing the departure. But there is also the other side of the transition: preparation for the move to a new position. It is not only a transition *from*, it is also a transition *to*. What might be the next call?

Hearing the Next Call

Discerning a new call often requires guidance from those around us, especially our mentors who know us well and are seeking the Lord's purposes for our lives.

It can also help to remember those things we might use to guide others in their discernment of a move, such as attending to your heart's desires, identifying your gifting, and considering the level of leadership for which you are prepared.

Discovering what the Lord has laid on your heart (Ps 37:4) is often a challenge. It involves seeing what you feel *passionate* about. Willow Creek's Network Course recommends trying to discover passions by asking questions such as, "What would you stay up late at night talking about?" Exercises like this might help you see where you would be able to serve best. It is about seeking to discern "where our deep gladness meets the world's deep need," as Frederick Buechner puts it.[12] It might also be a matter of looking at various possibilities, seeing what catches your attention, and asking God to open the right door for you. Often it is only when you visit a church or organization that you get a sense of God's call to that place as you feel a love for those people. In fact, if you do not feel a love for them, it might not be your call.

It can be very helpful to develop this thinking further using the *vision, purpose and core values* paradigm that we discussed in Phase 3. How might you describe yourself if you were doing what you believe God has called and equipped you to do – in other words, what is your personal vision? What would then be at the heart of what you were doing – your overall purpose in life? And what are the things you hold dearest that motivate you to want to do these things and guide how you do them – in other words, your core values? There is an exercise at the end of Phase 3 which provides a way of putting these pieces together. Francis Barongo, Archdeacon of Kitari Diocese, Uganda, shared an example of this on page 51. Those insights may well help you clarify the search. They will also serve you well for leadership in general, especially when you face setbacks.[13] In fact, being able to articulate what you think your life is all about, as far as you can discern it, brings clarity and focus to all aspects of your life, which offers numerous benefits. Rob Goffee and Gareth Jones go so far as to say, "Unless you are clear about your purpose and your values and are doing something that you really care about, it is difficult to act as a leader."[14]

Attending to your *gifts* is a second important facet of discerning a call. Presumably, one of your gifts is leadership, whether the natural gift, the spiritual gift (Rom 12:8), or both. Either way, this is a gift to be exercised

12. Frederick Buechner, *Wishful Thinking: A Theological ABC* (New York: Harper & Row, 1973), 95.

13. Seligman, "Building Resilience," 33–34, where values in particular are identified as helping build resilience.

14. Rob Goffee and Gareth Jones, *Why Should Anyone Be Led by You? What It Takes to Be an Authentic Leader* (Boston: Harvard Business Review Press, 2019), 73, italics removed.

and nurtured. But what about your other gifts? Do you have a special gift for teaching, for evangelism, or for service in areas of social justice? Noticing where God has gifted you can help guide you as you look for your next call, so long as you remember that leadership is not to be driven by meeting one's own needs. As leadership coach Mary Hays says, "Christian leadership is about self-abandonment, not self-fulfilment."[15]

The third aspect of seeking the next place of leadership is evaluating where you are in terms of developing your *leadership skills*. What challenge might you be ready to undertake next? As a general rule, there are some roles that you can take on in your first decade of leadership, others in the second, and still others in the third and fourth. At each stage you are, we hope, growing in Christlike character, becoming better able to recognize other leaders, learning how to discern vision and to implement plans to bring it about, and developing wise judgement, steady courage and proper humility. You should have better people skills and stronger financial management abilities, and make more effective use of time. You have also probably grown in patience, persistence and resilience. In addition, you may well have a greater sense of far-sightedness, and more gravitas. This all requires experience. So there are ministries, churches, departments or organizations you could probably lead now that you were not ready to lead ten years ago. It is not about promotion in the worldly sense. In fact, taking what might be regarded as a demotion can serve to check any pride that might be growing up within us, which could undermine our leadership capacity. It is, however, to acknowledge that, by God's grace, leaders generally get better at leading as they go along, and it is wise to seek to continue following the trajectory God is taking you on. The key thing is the desire to do God's will and be willing to do whatever God calls you to do, whether it seems greater or smaller, remembering that God looks on the heart (1 Sam 16:7).

Preparing for the Next Call

A transition like this is an opportunity for further development as a godly leader. Ideally, there should be some *time between calls*, at least to make any necessary housing move and to have a break or take a holiday. Simon Walker recommends something more substantial: stepping out of leadership itself every five years or so to see whether we are truly free to lead, or have become

15. This was part of a personal conversation with Mary Hays about leadership transitions.

dependent on a leadership role to define who we are.[16] Without intending to do so, I have experienced such breaks from leadership myself. Between leading a church for six years and leading a theological college, I had three years as a faculty member. After eight years leading a theological college I am now in an assistant leader role, albeit still on a senior leadership team. I can see that these times have been very good for me, and I am deeply grateful for them. They have provided fresh perspectives on leadership, and helped me grow as a leader. Such extended breaks from an overall leadership position are hard to plan and may be impractical for many, but a sabbatical time between jobs or every seven years or so in a leadership role can provide many of the same benefits. Such things provide a chance to stand back and notice things we are normally too busy to see, and to check we are leading for the sake of others and not for the sake of ourselves.

It is good to take this opportunity to *reflect on what you have learned about leadership* in this last season. What would you do differently if you had your time over again? If you keep a journal, this is a good moment to review past entries, noticing any patterns that emerge, positive or negative, that could affect your future leadership. This exercise might also help you to navigate the disorientation of any such transition, since there does need to be a letting go of what you were doing before you can arrive at a new beginning. It is an uncomfortable time and has been helpfully named "the neutral zone" of uncertainty by William Bridges, who has made a study of these transitions.[17]

One particularly valuable checklist for any leader at this transitional point is provided by Christian businessman and author Max De Pree in *Leadership Is an Art.* He says:[18]

1. Leaders should leave behind them assets (money, buildings and people) and a legacy.
2. Leaders are obligated to provide and maintain momentum.
3. Leaders are responsible for effectiveness.
4. Leaders must take a role in developing, expressing and defending civility and values.

16. Simon P. Walker, *Leading out of Who You Are: Discovering the Secret of Undefended Leadership* (Carlisle: Piquant, 2007), 156.

17. William Bridges, *Managing Transitions: Making the Most of Change*, 4th ed. (Boston: Da Capo Lifelong Books, 2017).

18. Max De Pree, *Leadership Is an Art* (New York: Doubleday, 1989), 13–22.

No doubt all of us fall short on one or more of these, but taking time to reflect on how true these things were of your recent leadership could be valuable as you prepare for the next call, and think what you might want to do differently in the future. It is worth noticing how much of this is about relationships. As Kouzes and Posner observe, it is the "quality of our relationships that most determine[s] whether our legacy will be ephemeral or lasting."[19] And they point out that people remember best what you did for them, not for yourself.[20] How marvellous if we could all say with the prophet Samuel,

> "Here I am; testify against me before the LORD and before his anointed. Whose ox have I taken? Or whose donkey have I taken? Or whom have I defrauded? Whom have I oppressed? Or from whose hand have I taken a bribe to blind my eyes with it? Testify against me and I will restore it to you." They said, "You have not defrauded us or oppressed us or taken anything from the hand of anyone." He said to them, "The LORD is witness against you, and his anointed is witness this day, that you have not found anything in my hand." And they said, "He is witness." (1 Sam 12:3–5)

One striking *legacy* was that of the German Lutheran minister George Müller, who became the founder and director of five orphan houses in Bristol, England, accommodating over two thousand orphaned boys and girls. The houses were run on the basis of complete dependence on God for their daily supplies. In addition to the children who benefited from his care, the houses bore witness to the faith they represented. According to his biographer Nancy Garton, one of Müller's chief desires was to have something as a "visible proof, that God is willing and able, at the present day, to help those who rely upon Him."[21] That hope continues to be realized as the story is told of his remarkable example of faith. It had a significant effect on us at Trinity School for Ministry as we trusted God for financial provision, and saw to our great delight how we ended every year breaking even or with a surplus, often as the result of unexpected last-minute gifts. Since the financial year ended on 30 June, it became known as "the June miracle."

Leadership experts Rob Goffee and Gareth Jones recommend *getting feedback from others* to help leaders grow in their leadership. The goal of

19. Quoted by Blackaby, *Spiritual Leadership*, 359.

20. Quoted by Blackaby, 359.

21. Nancy Garton, *George Müller and His Orphans* (London: Hodder & Stoughton, 1963), 56.

leadership, as they see it, is to "be yourself – more – with skill."[22] From a Christian standpoint, this is about enabling us as leaders to be authentically who God has made us to be, and to keep on developing the skills we need to lead. "Great leaders are never finished," Goffee and Jones say. "All of us are challenged to constantly review and renew our leadership skills. Again, this is not an entirely individual task. Effective leadership development is fuelled by honest, authentic conversations with others. And honesty in many organisations is in short supply."[23] To grow as leaders, we need reliable feedback about how we are doing. It would be helpful to know how well others think we do with establishing trust, cultivating leaders, discerning vision and implementing plans. That should generate the kind of feedback that will help us know where our strengths and weaknesses lie, so that we can play to our strengths and address our weaknesses. Even in a Christian context, many people may be reluctant to be open with us in the normal course of life, perhaps out of concern for seeming disloyal or ungrateful. However, at such transitional moments, those reservations might be reduced so that greater openness is possible, which could be very helpful. Ideally, this would be 360 degree feedback, coming from those above, beside and below us in the organization.

This is also a time to *review all aspects of your ministry*, whether that includes preaching, teaching or pastoring, in addition to the leadership role. Have you become stale in any of these things? Where do you want, or need, to grow? Spending time with the Lord, and with others who know you well, might help you to see where you could usefully invest time in reading or taking classes. It could also be an opportunity to develop your leadership or management skills. There are many books and courses which could be helpful here. It is worth the investment of time and money to grow in these areas. I would, of course, recommend considering further study in a theological college that could help you in your future leadership.

Most importantly, *invest in your spiritual life*. Spend time in the Bible and in prayer, attend conferences that refresh and encourage you, undertake a retreat or spend time with those who will pray with you. Whatever those things are that help you come close to the Lord, make time for them and be still in God's presence. Nothing will strengthen you as a leader more than maturing in your relationship with your Father in heaven, through your union with Jesus Christ, and in the power of the Holy Spirit. That is how you renew the trustworthiness that is so fundamental to your leadership.

---

22. Goffee and Jones, *Why Should Anyone Be Led by You?*, 17.

23. Goffee and Jones, xi.

Maybe this is your last transition out of leadership and you are *retiring*. By this point you may have acquired a great deal of wisdom and experience. I hope you will be able to share them with those who are still practising as leaders. It was a great help to me to have the listening ear of senior leaders, some of whom were retired, available to hear what was going on in the work I was doing and to offer their advice and prayer support. Many times I could look back on what might have been mistakes or oversights that I was delivered from through their insights. Retired leaders have a great deal to give.

Conclusion

Transitioning out is a complex process and it is hard to navigate skilfully. By being conscious of the importance of leaving well, you can bless those you have been serving by bringing things to a good conclusion and leaving them in a strong position for your successor. It is important to remember even from your early days that a transition time will come, so you can be thinking about where you wish to leave things when you go, and be working towards such a healthy situation. Knowing that such a time will arrive should also mean that you can pay close attention to what might lie ahead and seek to be a better leader in the next chapter of life, or, if you are retiring, how you might share what you have learned with others. All these things are hugely valuable services to the wider church and the organizations you serve, and will strengthen their leadership for the future.

Taking It Further

How might you grow as a leader in transitioning out?

1. How can you keep fresh so that you can serve as long as you should in your current position?

2. Are there steps you could take to increase your resilience?

3. What are you doing to ensure that major ministry areas have strong leadership?

4. How are you raising up future leaders for your own position and similar ones elsewhere?

5. When do you think it might be time to transition out of your current leadership role?

6. Who will help you discern when it is the Lord's timing for a move?

7. Do you have someone, or a team, in place who could provide calm and encouraging leadership to your congregation or organization when you leave? If not, what could be done about that?

8. How can you make your transitioning out as smooth as possible?

9. What might be suitable next steps for you?

10. What could you be doing now to prepare for your next call?

Conclusion

Christian leadership is a great privilege and a formidable challenge. It is really hard, and truly wonderful. It depends on a quality of character, a set of skills and a body of knowledge that take years to develop, and at every point, if we are honest, we can see room for growth. Who is sufficient for these things? How can we live up to this calling? The challenge can indeed seem overwhelming. But the rewards are great: a legacy of people who have grown in maturity, an organization that is stronger than it was, and a greater confidence in the majesty and power of God. The apostle Paul could say the church he had established in Philippi was his "joy and crown" (Phil 4:1). If this is the Lord's calling, surely we must give ourselves to it in every possible way, and trust that the one who called us is faithful and will be with us all the way through.

What we have offered here is an overview of the different elements of leadership and how they are connected to each other, rather than an exhaustive account of leadership. There is more to be said about every aspect of what has been discussed here. The hope is that having a sense of the general shape of the seasons of leadership, the five phases of the leadership journey, will help considerably as we embrace this leadership call. It is important to know that building trust is the indispensable foundation of anything the leader does; little, if anything, can be done without it. It is also vital to realize that leaders need to cultivate other leaders in order to accomplish their purpose, so they should always be on the lookout for other potential leaders and try to develop them. With leaders being identified, and a senior leadership team established, you can together discern a vision for the future which will coordinate and inspire the efforts of all those involved with the church or organization. Then plans can be developed to move towards that vision, and those plans can be reviewed and renewed as necessary. Finally, there comes the time to leave and to transition out well. These are all typical aspects of leadership in any sphere, including Christian leadership, and it is a great asset to any leader to be aware of them.

One of the things that strikes me most, as I look back over my years leading St Helen's Church and Trinity School for Ministry, is the sheer divine serendipity of it – those delightful signs of God's providential care. Time and again, we were beneficiaries of unanticipated blessing. At St Helen's we saw that in contacting the consultant Laurence Gamlen, which led to the vision and purpose discernment that I didn't realize we needed; the conversation with the head teacher of the Montessori School that resulted in the redevelopment of the church hall; the failed attempt to restart St Francis Church that led to a much better plan; the provision of children's workers for St Helen's and St Francis Churches; and so much more. Then, at Trinity School for Ministry, there were countless examples of God bringing us just the right people and all the necessary provisions, especially financial provisions, at the very moment we needed them. It was in the normal course of everyday life and leadership that God was at work, doing more than I could ask or imagine. It was God who took the primary initiatives, not me. Yes, there were plenty of things that I had to do as a leader, but my main work was to pray and to ask God to take the lead. I remember talking with a retired Christian entrepreneur in Pittsburgh who was looking back over the years of what had been a very successful career in the computer industry. It had recently struck him that the two most significant things that had happened in that time simply fell into his lap. He could not in any sense claim they were his doing. He was just their beneficiary. That is my enduring sense of Christian leadership. It is what makes such leadership so truly marvellous and utterly awe-inspiring.

Even knowing all these things, however, the leadership task remains daunting. I still remember the first time I read *Spiritual Leadership* by J. Oswald Sanders as a teenager and thinking: Who is equipped to do all this? Sanders describes the dangers of false compromise, selfish ambition, discouraging failures, mood swings, jealousy and pride.[1] There is no doubt that the expectations are enormous and the risks high. The hardest part can be waiting to see prayers answered and reassuring ourselves and others that God is faithful and will do what is right. The invitation to be a leader is a call to keep growing up and becoming the faith-filled person God wants us to be. No one can do this in his or her own strength. We can, and must, rely on God's faithfulness, and the empowerment of the Holy Spirit. There is an invitation to prayer that captures the need well: "You cannot bear the weight of this calling in your own strength but only by the grace and power of God. Pray therefore that your heart may daily be enlarged and your understanding of the Scriptures enlightened. Pray earnestly for the gift of the Holy Spirit."[2]

For those of us who have the privilege of being called to leadership, surrounded by those who pray for us and support us in this work, what else

1. J. Oswald Sanders, *Spiritual Leadership* (Bromley: STL, 1967), 142–152.

2. Prayer for those about to be ordained in *Common Worship Ordination Services* (London: Church House, 2000).

can we say other than thanks be to God for such a high calling? It is a story-rich life, and it builds a strong and confident faith in Jesus Christ (1 Tim 3:13). The opportunities to do a great deal of good and to bring God's blessing to many people are so numerous that the role of the Christian leader is one that should be marked by thankfulness that we have been called to it. May the Holy Spirit strengthen us through every phase of leadership in every place where we serve, and use us to display the Lord's glory.

Glossary

Since the examples I use come largely from the Anglican/Episcopal world in which I serve, I include a short glossary here for those unfamiliar with that tradition.

Archdeacon: a senior ordained leader who assists a bishop with the administration of an area of a diocese.
Bishop: the most senior ordained leader of a diocese, or of a region within a diocese.
Church Council or Parochial Church Council: a committee elected by members of a congregation to manage the financial affairs of the church, maintain its assets, and promote the mission of the church.
Churchwarden: a senior church leader (not ordained).
Clergy: ordained ministers.
Confirmation: a service at which candidates confirm their faith in Jesus Christ, have hands laid on them for empowerment by the Holy Spirit, and offer themselves in the Lord's service.
Curate: an ordained leader serving as an assistant in a church where he or she can be mentored.
Diocese: a district under the supervision of a senior bishop.
Gift Day: a day set aside for people to make special offerings for the Lord's work.
Parish: the geographical area under the care of a vicar or rector.
Principal: the head of a college, who might be called a *President* in other contexts.
Theological College: a college that might be called a *Seminary* or *Bible College* in other contexts, which prepares people for Christian leadership, including ordained ministry.
Vicar or Rector: the ordained leader of a church or group of churches.
Vice-Principal: the assistant head of a college, who might be called a *Vice-President* in other contexts.

Further Reading

Beasley-Murray, Paul. *A Call to Excellence: An Essential Guide to Christian Leadership.* London: Hodder & Stoughton, 1995.

Blackaby, Henry, and Richard Blackaby. *Spiritual Leadership*. Revised edition. Nashville: Broadman & Holman, 2011.

Blanchard, Ken, and Phil Hodges. *The Servant Leader.* Nashville: Word, 2001.

Blanchard, Kenneth, and Spencer Johnson. *The One Minute Manager.* London: Fontana, 1983.

Bridges, William. *Managing Transitions: Making the Most of Change.* 4th edition. Boston: Da Capo Lifelong Books, 2017.

Britton, Anne, and Chris Waterston. *Financial Accounting.* 4th edition. Harlow: Pearson, 2006.

Buckingham, Marcus, and Curt Coffman. *First, Break All the Rules: What the World's Greatest Managers Do Differently.* London: Simon & Schuster, 1999.

Buechner, Frederick. *Wishful Thinking: A Theological ABC.* New York: Harper & Row, 1973.

Busby, Dan. *Trust: The Firm Foundation for Kingdom Fruitfulness.* Winchester, VA: ECFA, 2015.

Christensen, Clayton M. "How Will You Measure Your Life?" Harvard Business Review, *HBR's 10 Must Reads on Managing Yourself.* Boston: Harvard Business Review Press, 2010.

Coleman, Robert. *The Master Plan of Evangelism.* 2nd edition. Ada, MI: Revell, 2010.

Collins, Jim. *Good to Great.* New York: HarperCollins, 2001.

Collins, Jim, and Jerry I. Porras. *Built to Last: Successful Habits of Visionary Companies.* New York: HarperCollins, 1994.

Covey, Stephen R. *The Seven Habits of Highly Effective People.* New York: Simon & Schuster, 1989.

Covey, Stephen M. R., with Rebecca R. Merrill. *The Speed of Trust: The One Thing That Changes Everything.* New York: Free Press, 2006.

Croft, Steven. *The Gift of Leadership – According to the Scriptures.* Norwich: Canterbury Press, 2016.

De Pree, Max. *Leadership Is an Art.* New York: Doubleday, 1989.

———. *Leadership Jazz.* New York: Doubleday, 1992.

Drucker, Peter F. *The Essential Drucker: The Best of Sixty Years of Peter Drucker's Essential Writings on Management.* New York: Harper, 2001.

———. *The Practice of Management.* New York: Harper & Row, 1954.

Fernando, Ajith. *An Authentic Servant: The Marks of a Spiritual Leader.* 2nd edition. Leyland: 10publishing, 2007.

Finney, John. *Understanding Leadership.* London: Daybreak, 1989.

Fisher, Roger, and William Ury, with Bruce Patton. *Getting to Yes: Negotiating Agreement without Giving In*. 2nd edition. New York: Penguin, 1991.

Ford, Leighton. *Transforming Leadership: Jesus' Way of Creating Vision, Shaping Values and Empowering Change*. Downers Grove, IL: IVP Books, 1991.

Friedman, Edwin H. *A Failure of Nerve: Leadership in the Age of the Quick Fix*. New York: Seabury, 1997.

———. *Generation to Generation: Family Process in Church and Synagogue*. New York: Guilford Press, 1985.

Garton, Nancy. *George Müller and His Orphans*. London: Hodder & Stoughton, 1963.

Goffee, Rob, and Gareth Jones. *The Character of a Corporation: How Your Company's Culture Can Make or Break Your Business*. 2nd edition. London: Profile, 2003.

Goffee, Rob, and Gareth Jones. *Why Should Anyone Be Led by You? What It Takes to Be an Authentic Leader*. Boston: Harvard Business Review Press, 2019.

Goleman, Daniel. "What Makes a Leader?" *Harvard Business Review* 82, no. 1 (January 2004): 82–91.

Goossen, Richard J., and R. Paul Stevens. *Entrepreneurial Leadership: Finding Your Calling, Making a Difference*. Downers Grove, IL: InterVarsity Press, 2013.

Green, Michael. *Radical Leadership in the New Testament and Today*. London: SPCK, 2017.

Greenleaf, Robert K. *The Servant as Leader*. Cambridge, MA: Center for Applied Studies, 1973.

Guest, John. *Beating Mediocrity: Six Habits of the Highly Effective Christian*. Grand Rapids, MI: Baker, 1993.

Handy, Charles. *The Age of Unreason*. London: Random House, 1991.

———. *Understanding Voluntary Organizations*. London: Penguin, 1988.

Harle, Tim. *Leading in a Second Chair: Insights for First- and Second-Chair Leaders*. Cambridge: Grove Books, 2019.

Hartwig, Ryan T., and Warren Bird. *Teams That Thrive: Five Disciplines of Collaborative Church Leadership*. Downers Grove, IL: InterVarsity Press, 2015.

Harvard Business Review. *HBR's 10 Must Reads on Emotional Intelligence*. Boston: Harvard Business Review Press, 2015.

———. *HBR's 10 Must Reads on Leadership*. Boston: Harvard Business Review Press, 2011.

———. *HBR's 10 Must Reads on Managing People*. Boston: Harvard Business Review Press, 2011.

———. *HBR's 10 Must Reads on Managing Yourself*. Boston: Harvard Business Review Press, 2010.

———. *HBR's 10 Must Reads on Mental Toughness*. Boston: Harvard Business Review Press, 2018.

———. *HBR's 10 Must Reads on Strategy*. Boston: Harvard Business Review Press, 2011.

Harvey-Jones, John. *Making It Happen: Reflections on Leadership*. Glasgow: Collins, 1988.

Herman, Robert D., and Associates. *The Jossey-Bass Handbook of Nonprofit Leadership and Management*. 2nd edition. San Francisco: Jossey-Bass, 2005.

Hesselbein, Frances, Marshall Goldsmith, and Richard Beckhard, eds. *The Leaders of the Future*. San Francisco: Jossey-Bass, 1996.

Jackson, Bob. *Hope for the Church: Contemporary Strategies for Growth*. London: Church House, 2002.

———. *The Road to Growth: Towards a Thriving Church*. London: Church House, 2005.

Kamau, Ken. *First Things First: Growing in Pastoral Ministry*. Nairobi: HippoBooks, 2016.

King, Philip. *Leadership Explosion: Maximising Leadership Potential in the Church*. London: Hodder & Stoughton, 1987.

Kotter, John. *Leading Change*. Boston: Harvard Business Press, 2012.

Kouzes, James, and Barry Posner. *The Leadership Challenge: How to Make Extraordinary Things Happen in Organizations*. 5th edition. San Francisco: Wiley, 2012.

Lafley, A. G., and Roger L. Martin. *Playing to Win: How Strategy Really Works*. Boston: Harvard Business Review Press, 2013.

Laughlin, Patrick R., Erin C. Hatch, Jonathan S. Silver, and Lee Boh. "Groups Perform Better Than the Best Individuals on Letters-to-Numbers Problems: Effects of Group Size." *Journal of Personality and Social Psychology* 90, no. 4 (2006): 644–651.

Lawrence, James. *Growing Leaders: Reflections on Leadership, Life and Jesus*. Abingdon: Bible Reading Fellowship, 2004.

Legge, Peter. *The Power of Tact 2.0*. Burnaby, BC: Eaglet, 2018.

Lencioni, Patrick M. *The Five Dysfunctions of a Team: A Leadership Fable*. San Francisco: Jossey-Bass, 2002.

Lombardo, Michael M., and Robert W. Eichinger. *The Career Architect Development Planner*. 1st edition. Minneapolis: Lominger, 1996.

MacArthur, John. *Called to Lead: Lessons from the Life of the Apostle Paul*. Nashville: Nelson, 2004.

Maxwell, John C. *The 21 Irrefutable Laws of Leadership: Follow Them and People Will Follow You*. Nashville: Thomas Nelson, 1998.

Mead, Loren B. *Five Challenges for the Once and Future Church*. Herndon, VA: Alban Institute, 1996.

Mullins, Laurie J. *Management and Organisational Behaviour*. 10th edition. Harlow: FT Publishing, 2013.

Neill, Stephen. *The Christian Character*. London: United Society for Christian Literature, 1955.

Nelson, John, ed. *Management and Ministry*. Norwich: Canterbury Press, 1996.

Newbigin, Lesslie. *The Gospel in a Pluralist Society*. London: SPCK, 1989.

Nouwen, Henri. *A Spirituality of Fundraising*. Nashville: Upper Room Books, 2010.

Parkinson, Ian. *Enabling Succession*. Cambridge: Grove Books, 2017.

———. *Understanding Christian Leadership*. London: SCM, 2020.

Peters, Thomas J., and Robert H. Waterman Jr. *In Search of Excellence: Lessons from America's Best-Run Companies*. New York: Harper & Row, 1982.

Peters, Tom. *Thriving on Chaos: A Handbook for a Management Revolution*. New York: Harper & Row, 1988.

Peters, Tom, and Nancy Austin. *A Passion for Excellence: The Leadership Difference*. New York: Collins, 1985.

Piggott, Andy. *Leaving Well: Exploring Aspects of Moving from One Ministry to Another*. Cambridge: Grove Books, 2014.

Pytches, David. *Leadership for New Life*. London: Hodder & Stoughton, 1998.

Rayburn, Robert S., and Steven A. Nicoletti. "An Elder Must Have Believing Children: Titus 1:6 and a Neglected Case of Conscience." *Presbyterion* 43, no. 2 (Fall 2017): 69–80.

Rinehart, John. *Gospel Patrons: People Whose Generosity Changed the World*. Fullerton, CA: Reclaimed Publishing, 2013.

Roxburgh, Alan J., and Fred Romanuk. *The Missional Leader: Equipping Your Church to Reach a Changing World*. San Francisco: Jossey-Bass, 2006.

Saïdi, Farida. *A Study of Current Leadership Styles in the North African Church*. Carlisle: Langham Monographs, 2013.

Sanders, J. Oswald. *Spiritual Leadership*. Bromley: STL, 1967.

Schein, Edgar H. *Organizational Culture and Leadership*. 2nd edition. San Francisco: Jossey-Bass, 1992.

Seligman, Martin. *Learned Optimism*. Boston: Nicholas Brearley, 2018.

Senge, Peter M. *The Fifth Disciple: The Art and Practice of the Learning Organization*. Revised edition. New York: Doubleday, 2006.

Shawchuck, Norman, and Roger Heuser. *Leading the Congregation*. Nashville: Abingdon, 1993.

Shawchuck, Norman, and Roger Heuser. *Managing the Congregation*. Nashville: Abingdon, 1996.

Sinek, Simon. *Start with Why: How Great Leaders Inspire Everyone to Take Action*. New York: Penguin, 2009.

Stanley, Andy. *Making Vision Stick*. Grand Rapids, MI: Zondervan, 2007.

Stott, John. *Calling Christian Leaders: Biblical Models of Church, Gospel and Ministry*. Leicester: Inter-Varsity Press, 2002.

———. *The Message of 1 Timothy and Titus*. Leicester: Inter-Varsity Press, 1998.

Temple, William. *Readings in John's Gospel*. New York: Morehouse, 1985.

Tracy, Brian. *Leadership*. New York: Amacom, 2014.

———. *Management*. New York: Amacom, 2014.

Walker, Simon P. *Leading Out of Who You Are: Discovering the Secret of Undefended Leadership*. Carlisle: Piquant, 2007.

Warren, Rick. *The Purpose Driven Church: Growth without Compromising Your Message and Mission*. Grand Rapids, MI: Zondervan, 1995.

Weems, Lovett H. *Church Leadership: Vision, Team, Culture and Integrity*. Nashville: Abingdon Press, 1993.

Wright, Walter C. *Relational Leadership: A Biblical Model for Leadership Service*. Carlisle: Paternoster, 2000.

Subject Index

Scripture Index

OLD TESTAMENT

NEW TESTAMENT

Langham Literature and its imprints are a ministry of Langham Partnership.

Langham Partnership is a global fellowship working in pursuit of the vision God entrusted to its founder John Stott –

> ***to facilitate the growth of the church in maturity and Christ-likeness through raising the standards of biblical preaching and teaching.***

Our vision is to see churches in the Majority World equipped for mission and growing to maturity in Christ through the ministry of pastors and leaders who believe, teach and live by the word of God.

Our mission is to strengthen the ministry of the word of God through:
- nurturing national movements for biblical preaching
- fostering the creation and distribution of evangelical literature
- enhancing evangelical theological education

especially in countries where churches are under-resourced.

Our ministry

Langham Preaching partners with national leaders to nurture indigenous biblical preaching movements for pastors and lay preachers all around the world. With the support of a team of trainers from many countries, a multi-level programme of seminars provides practical training, and is followed by a programme for training local facilitators. Local preachers' groups and national and regional networks ensure continuity and ongoing development, seeking to build vigorous movements committed to Bible exposition.

Langham Literature provides Majority World preachers, scholars and seminary libraries with evangelical books and electronic resources through publishing and distribution, grants and discounts. The programme also fosters the creation of indigenous evangelical books in many languages, through writer's grants, strengthening local evangelical publishing houses, and investment in major regional literature projects, such as one volume Bible commentaries like *The Africa Bible Commentary* and *The South Asia Bible Commentary*.

Langham Scholars provides financial support for evangelical doctoral students from the Majority World so that, when they return home, they may train pastors and other Christian leaders with sound, biblical and theological teaching. This programme equips those who equip others. Langham Scholars also works in partnership with Majority World seminaries in strengthening evangelical theological education. A growing number of Langham Scholars study in high quality doctoral programmes in the Majority World itself. As well as teaching the next generation of pastors, graduated Langham Scholars exercise significant influence through their writing and leadership.

To learn more about Langham Partnership and the work we do visit **langham.org**

Lightning Source UK Ltd.
Milton Keynes UK
UKHW021303130521
383659UK00008B/1201